STUDENTS ON THE MARGINS

SUNY series Urban Voices, Urban Visions
Diane DuBose Brunner and Rashidah Jaami' Muhammad,
Editors

STUDENTS ON THE MARGINS

EDUCATION, STORIES, DIGNITY

Jaylynne N. Hutchinson

State University of New York Press

Published by
State University of New York Press, Albany

© 1999 State University of New York

Printed in the United States of America

For information, address State University of New York Press,
State University Plaza, Albany, N.Y. 12246

Production by Dale Cotton
Marketing by Anne M. Valentine

Library of Congress Cataloging-in-Publication Data

Hutchinson, Jaylynne N., 1954–
    Students on the margins : education, stories, dignity / by
Jaylynne N. Hutchinson.
       p.   cm. — (SUNY series, urban voices, urban visions)
    Includes bibliographical references (p.   ) and index.
    ISBN 0-7914-4165-2 (alk. paper). — ISBN 0-7914-4166-0 (pbk. :
alk. paper)
    1. Education—United States—Philosophy. 2. Educational change—
United States. 3. Moral education—United States. 4. Students—
United States. I. Title. II. Series.
LA210.H88   1999
370'.1—dc21
                                        98-33675
                                         CIP

10 9 8 7 6 5 4 3 2 1

to my parents
upon whose shoulders I stand

and

to my children
for the journey we share

CONTENTS

PREFACE

Much is expected of our schools, perhaps too much, or more carefully said, perhaps the wrong things. How then, do we decide what it is that most needs our attention? The purpose of writing this book is to explore the notion that by not paying attention to the core stories of our students' lives, we miss reaching the space where they truly experience growth. To reach this space we must access where our students make meaning. It is a complicated process that requires paying attention to the whole self, not just to the cognitive domain. It requires paying attention to what Jane Roland Martin calls the "three C's" of care, concern, and connection. But if schools are in the business simply of filling up young minds with facts, then the "banking" model that Paulo Freire warns us about will suffice. If schools are in the business of turning out people-widgets to keep our country competitive in a global economy, then the traditional factory model of schooling will suffice where teachers are the line workers, each doing his or her discrete task of information depositing as the students pass through, year by year, semester by semester, along the assembly line we call "school." But although we often find ourselves, especially in secondary

and higher education, operating with such a model, it is not a model
that many teachers or students enjoy or want.

I often begin my classes for students who are preparing to be
teachers and educational leaders by creating a list of the powerful
things we ourselves liked about school and what we did not like.
Students then read about the two schooling experiences of bell hooks
that I describe in chapter 7, and perhaps, look at how Paulo Freire
characterizes "banking" education juxtaposed with "problem posing"
education. Invariably, the list we make of the positive and powerful
features of our education includes being known, teachers caring
about you, relevant subject material, sense of belonging, hard work,
fun, learning a lot, having choices, lively discussions, projects, the
arts, critical thinking, finding a "voice," having someone believe in
you, connecting to the community and to one's family, talking about
things that "really matter." Perhaps you know this list. It often represents the teacher we think of when asked, "What teacher really
impacted your life?"

On the list of things that describe what we did not like about
school, students complain that school is boring, anonymous, the
material is irrelevant, passive, no choice or self-direction, mean teachers, learning nothing, forgetting what was just memorized, being
lectured at, only reading and writing, grades more important than
anything, not being respected, unfair rules, taking tests, and you
know the rest! As a class, we look at the lists we have created on the
blackboard. We are satisfied with what is represented under each
category. Then I ask three questions. First, "As you look at the board,
what kind of schooling experience did you enjoy the most?" Obvi-
ously, students clamor that they liked school when it matched the list
of positive and powerful things about education. But, sadly, we note
that for most of us this powerfully educative experience did not
happen very often throughout the years we spent in school. Second,
I ask, "What kind of teacher would you want to be?" Students look
at me as if this were a "no-brainer." Of course, there seems to be an
obvious answer to this question. They want to be the kind of teacher
that engenders that first column of positive and powerful student
responses to education. The third question does not produce the
same clamoring response. I ask, "If it is true that as both a student
and a teacher you want to create a powerful and positive educational
experience called "schooling," and if we assume that sitting here
today preparing to be teachers and educational leaders, we feel pretty

much like most individuals who choose and have chosen teaching as their profession, how is it that overwhelmingly our educational experiences fall under the list we labeled as negative school experiences? At their silence I probe further. What happens between the time you sit here in these chairs with an understanding of what it means to have a teacher who touches your life, knowing exactly what a powerful and moving educational experience is, and the time that you become the type of teacher who engenders the list our class created of educational negatives that most of us say characterizes the majority of our schooling? This is when the important dialogue begins.

Some might criticize me for dwelling on the negatives. I respond that my intent is to point out the contradictions between what we hope for and what we often do. The purpose of this book is not to be critical of teachers, that profession of which I am a part, but to peel away the layers of the onion, carefully examining what often occurs in the everyday lived experience of how we "do" school. It is a compelling and troublesome question to ask how is it that we, as educators, want the best, most exciting learning experiences for the students in our classes, but have many of our students walk away feeling on the margins of what happens in schools? It is my hopeful and optimistic belief that teachers *want* to create powerfully educative experiences for their students. The problem is that we have not created an educational system that allows that to happen on a regular basis. It is an indictment of how we "do" education that we even ask that age-old question, "What teacher has most impacted your life?" Every teacher should! That is the hope of almost every teacher I have met. Acknowledging that these are our best intents as educators, the questions that then face us are why, even with our best intentions, do our students not find school engaging, challenging, compelling, and joyous, and how can we remedy this?

It serves only the interests of the status quo to dismiss this conversation as negative and critical of teachers. Rather, in writing this book, I envision a rich sense of freedom for teachers and students. In *Releasing the Imagination*, Maxine Greene teaches us that we can gain this sense of freedom

only when what presses down (or conditions or limits) is perceived as an obstacle. Where oppression or exploitation or pollution or even pestilence is perceived as natural, as a given, there can be no freedom. Where people cannot name alternatives or

> imagine a better state of things, they are likely to remain an-
> chored or submerged. If we teachers are to develop a humane
> and liberating pedagogy, we must feel ourselves to be engaged in
> a dialectical relation. (52)

Drawing our attention to such an everyday lived contradiction is an
impetus to imagining the world of school, of teaching, of learning,
in a different way. For until we are able to imagine, it cannot be.

I propose that the terms of our debate about educational reform
are misplaced. Our educational dialogue must put the domain of the
moral at the forefront or the foundation of other instrumental, structural, methological, and curricular discussions, and not the other
way around. We cannot address the moral only if we find time for it.
If we begin with the moral, we eventually will get to the others, but
if we begin with these other facets of our educational day, we will not
necessarily arrive at the moral. If we were to measure our educational proposals against how well the dignity of all our children might
be sustained or helped to flourish, perhaps our schools would look
different indeed. And perhaps teachers would finally be able to act
upon the desires and intents that brought them to teaching in the
first place. Although this book primarily explores the moral and
educational importance of paying attention to students' core stories,
a companion volume could and should be written about teachers'
voices and stories!

This book does not purport a recipe for school success. It asks
us, as educators, parents, and other adults who care about what
happens to children to examine the implications of how we teach,
how we are with the students in our classes, and to look at where we
create spaces for students to bring themselves to the journey of learning. Perhaps as a preparatory question, we need to ask ourselves,
where are the spaces wherein we as teachers can bring ourselves to
our teaching and learning? I invite you to reflect upon Walker Percy's
quotation at the beginning of this book. Teachers are presented with
many methods and theories of learning and development. All of
these are necessary. But in the spirit of Percy, teachers also "live out
the rest of the day" in classrooms with students of all sorts of backgrounds, learning styles, behaviors, motivations, and interests and
with all sorts of parents, socio-economic backgrounds, and languages.
This is the realm that Percy called the "not entirely" that our theories do not address. Yet this is the realm wherein the most powerful
and educative experiences often occur. It is the realm of the moral,

the realm of meaning, the realm of identity, the realm of growth. It is to this realm that we must turn our educational dialogue so that children's lives can flourish as their education helps them imbue their lives with meaning. To do so is to pay attention to their dignity and their stories.

ACKNOWLEDGMENTS

This book represents many hours of reading and thinking and dialogue with peers and colleagues about critical issues that impact the well-being of children in our schools. This book also is a compilation of experiences and observations at schools and discussions with teachers who care deeply about what it is we "do" in schools. I am still amazed and inspired by the hope they have for our future. In addition, the life and educational experiences of many children inform the writing of this book. No author can disengage completely from their own experience (nor would I want to) and each colleague and teacher and student with whom I have spoken has added a piece of their own testimony to what school is and what it can become. In particular, I owe a special thanks to three wonderful teachers, Joyce Bonney, Kelly Joy, and Diane Loesch.

This work originated while I was at the University of Washington and I would like to thank those who opened the doors that allowed me to explore an issue that was of deep importance to me. Special thanks are due to Donna Kerr, Deborah Kerdeman, Robert Schultz, Husain Bashey, and Jamie Mayerfeld for their input and critique that has been helpful in shaping this work and making it better than where it began. In addition, the inspiration to continue working on this book has been kept alive through the support of those who began as peers, quickly turned into friends, and are now cherished colleagues. Their support keeps my hope alive!

I would like to thank the State University of New York Press for working with me in preparing this manuscript and the positive support I received from their editors and staff. I have learned that publishing requires patience and am grateful for their guidance through this process and their belief that this book has a story worth telling.

My children and my family and friends, and my students have kept me honest and for that I thank them and hope they see a reflection of their concerns in my writing. My hope is that where we find students on the margins, that we invite them in.

Excerpts from Thomas Green, "Unwrapping the Ordinary: Philosophical Projects" in *American Journal of Education,* November 1991, (Chicago: The University of Chicago Press, 1991).

Excerpts from Daniel Pekarsky, "Dehumanization and Education," *Teachers College Record* 84, no. 2, Winter 1987 (New York: Teachers College Record, 1987).

Excerpts from Thomas Green, "Public Speech," *18th Annual DeGarmo Lecture of the Society of Professors of Education.* (San Francisco: Caddo Gap Press, 1993).

Excerpts from bell hooks, *Teaching to Transgress: Education as the Practice of Freedom* (New York: Routledge, Inc., 1994).

1

IMAGINING EDUCATION:
The Questions We Ask

I would prefer to describe it as a certain view of man, an anthropology, if you like; of man as wayfarer, in a rather conscious contrast to prevailing views of man as organism, as enculturated creature, as consumer, Marxist, as subject to such-and-such a scientific or psychological understanding—all of which he is, but not entirely. It is the "not entirely" I'm interested in—like the man Kierkegaard described who read Hegel, understood himself and the universe perfectly by noon, but then had the problem of living out the rest of the day.

—Walker Percy, *Signpost in a Strange Land*

Why is it that educational problems plague us so? Could it be that educationally, we are like the individual Kierkegaard describes above, who seeks knowledge and understanding in the prolific body of educational research, but who then still has the problem of "living out the rest of the day" in school rooms, with diverse students, parents, and colleagues? In this book I propose that along with the

1

legitimate educational research that informs our practice, we are paying too little attention to certain elements in our inquiry that could speak to how we live out the rest of the day as we engage in educating. There are two characteristics of this inquiry that are critical to its efficacy in speaking to our educational lives. First, such an inquiry must be interdisciplinary in nature. Second, it must engage in a moral dialogue that merges theory and practice, the abstract and the particular. In doing so, it must recast our most intractable educational problems as energizing tensions, rather than as conflicts. I will address each of these characteristics in turn.

By its very nature, education is one of the most interdisciplinary activities of our lives. First, it brings persons together who often vary dramatically in age, race, class, gender, and authority. Each of these descriptors of ourselves brings with it varying and interactive lenses through which we view the world. Second, the process of education itself exists within an understanding of the *psychology* of how one changes and learns; the individual and age pattern development of the learner, as well as the psychology and emotion of the teacher; the *philosophy* of teaching in its aims and goals and the *ethics* of its delivery; the *sociology* of the institution of schooling, of the family and society who send their children to school, of demographic patterns of race, class, and gender; the *political science* of government influence in curricula and standards, of research and the *economics* of funding; the *history* of traditions and patterns that define educational practice. In each of these disciplines, there are two foci: a micro focus on the individual student, teacher, or school; and a macro focus on the larger society or overall practice of education. Education is inherently interdisciplinary and at some point, must create an interdisciplinary conversation when addressing itself as a whole.

In most of the universities that house colleges of education, one often finds many disciplines represented, that is, historians of education, curriculum specialists, economic researchers, sociologists, administrators, and more. Yet they often have little to do with one another in their professional work. Philosophers of education write for and attend conferences with other philosophers of education, secondary math teachers write for and attend conferences with other secondary math teachers, administrators write for and attend conferences with other administrators, and preservice teacher candidates pursue course work separate from counselor education and principal candidates even though they will all work together at a common site for a common purpose. This fragmentation continues throughout the university community with the scholars of each discipline laboring in their own field. There are many reasons why this is so, and I will not debate the merits of this fragmentation here, but I raise the issue to point to a deficit in our educational discourse. If the process of education is so utterly multifaceted, how can we be confident that we have addressed all that we must to enrich our praxis and improve the quality of education if we do not have an equally multifaceted discourse about these issues? In this work I attempt to bring a somewhat interdisciplinary lens to bear on the comments I make about the culture of education, which includes its theory and its practice. In this regard, my writing is not easily categorizable, nor is it easy to determine to which audience it should be directed. That is all as it should be.

What I hope to provide herein is a part of a conversation that is necessary in our attempts to talk about what is wrong or what is right with education today. Noted educational researcher John Goodlad has recently re-released a small book entitled *What Schools Are For*. In this book, Goodlad argues that we must "initiate a national dialogue about what education is, what it should do, and where it can be most productively advanced."[1] I assume that this dialogue is not simply another call for political leaders to grandstand on educational issues. Rather, such a dialogue must reflect the interdisciplinary nature of education by involving the parties most implicated in it's practice. Who would it include? Educators (both frontline classroom teachers and educational academics), parents of many varieties; students of many ages and backgrounds; community leaders, including government, business, *and* the arts. These conversations or dialogues must proceed along the lines of the slogan Think Globally, Act Locally. In other words, more expansive theory and careful, critical thinking must be called upon to inform the local concrete practice and context within which schools operate. One without the other is fragmentary and ultimately creates the person Kierkegaard described as being full of theory, but wondering still how to live.

Such a complaint is common among those preparing to be teachers. On occasion I assign Goodlad's book to a class of graduate preservice teachers. They bring the urgent demands of classroom practice to their reading of this book. While they are supportive of the need for a larger dialogue about education, they want to know what this might look like and how such a conversation could occur and be brought to bear on improving education. In other words, they want the conversation to reach beyond and perhaps even originate from places other than the political or higher education arenas. They are correct in wanting to know more. Before culminating in policy decisions, before being brought to a vote at a school board meeting, there must be much discussion on the purposes and implications of how we *do* school. These conversations must be more informal and occur where the stakes are not so high that we prematurely close the door on listening to others. And the conversations must be more inclusive of those who are implicated in the practice of schooling. Some cities have held "education summits," but these often are framed by the political arena, and many folks are precluded from participating. More grassroots and ultimately a necessity for community and parental support, are conversations that occur close to home. In some districts, principals offer to meet with groups of parents in their homes for dialogue about what is happening in their schools. Teachers invite parents and students to classroom picnics *before* the school year begins in order to develop a sense of inclusive community. Parents are invited into the schools in meaningful ways, participating on school decision-making committees or in the classroom, extending the traditional nursery school parent co-op commitment through the eighth grade. We need to imagine new ways to converse about education in a manner that prevents fractiousness.

Bringing an interdisciplinary lens to these conversations is the first step in synthesis which is a necessary prerequisite for addressing complex social issues. One interdisciplinary education program defines synthesis as the "ability to weave many complex strands into a fabric of definable issues, patterns, and topics."[2] With this book I attempt to enter into such an interdisciplinary conversation, drawing from the ideas, experiences, and work of others and myself in a process of synthesis.

The second characteristic of this inquiry is that it develops from my work in moral philosophy. In this introduction I place my work within a larger body of scholarly work regarding education. In addition, I describe the method by which I have joined in the educational conversation that addresses what schools *ought* to do and how they *should* be for our children. In so doing, this book contributes to an area of educational discourse that is often overlooked in dialogue regarding educational improvement and reform. Simply put, this book addresses the moral character of education and the relationships embedded therein. While scholars have written in this realm generally, the discussion of the moral nature of education in relation to educational renewal or reform is lacking in much of current educational discourse and policy. Consider the following two points.

My first point regards the general nature of this discourse. While it is true that there has been a body of writing on the moral nature of education, it generally takes two forms. Either the writing is all but encompassed within the realm of moral philosophy and lacks a connection to the practice of education, or the writing addresses the practice of education and educators, with an ancillary discussion of its moral dimension, and in so doing, it often lacks a breadth of moral complexity. In this work I attempt to bridge the gap between these two ways of addressing the moral nature of education. Accordingly, this book attempts to focus exclusively on fundamental moral questions regarding education, but does so in a way that constantly ties them to the phenomenological experience of educational practice.

My second point regards the specific nature of my topic. The notion of dignity is one that appears self-evident in its importance, and yet too often the everyday practice of education affronts the dignity of young people. With this in mind, I have undertaken a philosophical exploration to "unwrap the ordinary," a process that Thomas Green describes:

> Observe this progression—first, the ordinary, or "ordinary life," then comes philosophy as the occasionally intrusive reflection on the ordinary, and finally, if we wish to go even farther, there is philosophy as the record of that reflection. The thesis here is that doing philosophy, in contrast to merely studying it, especially in the case of education, is simply the task of unwrapping the ordinary. *It is making evident what we already know, but may have overlooked.* (Emphasis mine.)[3]

In this manner, I take the practice of education (a part of ordinary life to be sure) and ask if our self-evident acceptance of dignity is actually realized in our practice. Further, I ask, what would the nature of schooling be like if the sustaining and enhancing of children's dignity were a fundamental concern? To my knowledge, this question has not been addressed before, and, therefore, this book makes a contribution to understanding the moral character of education and educational practice. In this effort, I am not vilifying our teachers who labor day in and day out for the benefit of the children in our schools. As I often comment in my classes, I know of no teacher who sets out to harm children or who would choose to create an educational environment that dominates or stifles. But we all know children, perhaps even ourselves once, who have said, "School is boring!" "It's like a prison there!" "Nobody cares about me!" Interestingly enough, these complaints grow as students progress through the years. The question I pose to my students is, what shall we make of this situation? If teachers do not intend to harm children (and they do not), why are so many children unhappy and unengaged in our schools today? I believe that we must explore the moral nature of education in order to understand this paradox.

Scholars have written about different moral characteristics that are necessary to education. For example, in *Caring: A Feminine Approach to Ethics and Moral Education*, Nel Noddings thoughtfully outlines an ethic based on caring. In her book of approximately two hundred pages, roughly twenty pages address moral education. This is an example of a treatise in moral philosophy that addresses education as an ancillary concern. Alternatively, in *Lives on the Edge*, Valerie Polakow exposes the way that institutional social structures perpetuate inequities within education that contribute to a "pedagogy of the poor." While a concern for sustaining the dignity of children is apparent in her powerful book, its main focus is on the structural marginalization of poor and oppressed women and children in the United States today. Others have written in the subject domain of stories, but again the focus appears either to be on a deeply philosophical treatment of the subject or on a practical application of the role of stories in schools. Again, I attempt to bridge the gap by undertaking a conversation of moral philosophy that measures itself against the practice with which I am concerned.

Others have written similar work in different fields. For example, in the field of psychiatry, consider Robert Coles' *The Call of Stories: Teaching and the Moral Imagination*. This book explicated the role of stories in healing and the type of preparation that would assist doctors in becoming better, more caring physicians. Similarly, in the field of general medicine, Howard Brody's *Stories of Sickness* identifies the moral need for physicians to understand the role of stories in health and sickness in order to preserve the wholeness or dignity of an individual. I make a parallel claim within the context of education and address the specific role that stories play in preserving the dignity of children.

To do this I have drawn from the work of many others who have focused on notions that I employ to enrich the concepts of dignity, stories, and education. Among others, I draw upon the works of Charles Taylor regarding notions of authenticity, Maxine Greene and bell hooks regarding notions of freedom, and Thomas Green and Richard Rorty regarding notions of public discourse and ethics. In this way, my work is a synthesis of many outstanding contributions by thought-provoking philosophers of our day. I take their carefully articulated ideas and apply them to the process of "unwrapping the ordinary" in my discussion of dignity, stories, and education.

As we unwrap the layers of educational theory and practice, we begin to see some interesting things that will be helpful as we engage in educational conversations. At the root of most of the intractable problems in education, there are deep moral tensions.[4] These moral tensions often grow from contradictory social values that are etched deeply in the American psyche. These tensions have been observed and articulated by scholars such as de Tocqueville as he commented on the competing demands between individualism and the common good in American Society in *Democracy in America*. Lest we think these were only complications of a new nation, we can turn to Robert Bellah and colleagues who have examined this tension more fully in *Habits of the Heart*.[5] More recently, law professor Bruce Hafen identified schools as "mediating structures" in a democratic society. He describes this function:

> A school aspires to be a bridge between the private world of the individual and the public world of society, helping each individual to realize his own autonomous sense of self while simultaneously inducting him into membership in the democratic community. He (or she) thus learns to give as well as to take from the wellsprings of a free culture. To fulfill such contradictory but lofty purposes, the school as (a) mediating institution must itself be a paradoxical construct, belonging both to the private world of the family and to the public world of the state. Thus a school must reflect both institutional authority and personal autonomy, private values and public virtues, excellence and equality, neutrality and advocacy.[6]

For example, varied school debates about equity in funding or inclusion of students with disabilities go beyond the particular merits of a given proposal. Rather, at their base these dilemmas place us as individuals and as a society between our legitimate moral commitment to provide the best we can for our own children, *and* the lofty moral ideal of equality promised within our own larger community. Although these school debates seem to center on questions such as Do we have enough tax money to provide an equal education? or Is there enough teacher attention to go around when a child with a disability is placed within a classroom? these are not the real issues at stake that make these dilemmas appear intractable. The more fundamental questions that are rarely asked or addressed are questions such as Whose children are these? and How can I balance my commitment to myself (and mine) with my commitment to the larger good? Without acknowledging and addressing these kinds of foundational questions, we will go on ad infinitum in our debates. If we continue to cast the funding debate as the greedy, selfish rich on the one hand, and the lazy, uninspired poor on the other hand, then we will never find a way to address the severe funding and equity problem that haunts our childrens' education. In this regard, Hafen tells us that "the swings that have occurred in our educational history . . . are but manifestations of paradoxical conflicts between legitimate and competing principles that deal both with learning and with the important social purposes served by education."[7] Therefore, if, in our joint conversations, we can identify the competing pull of our moral commitments, then we can begin to discuss how to balance the equally valid moral commitments that parties bring to the educational table.

Hafen describes these tensions or contradictions as "productive and dynamic paradoxes that are inherent in the educational process."[8] For example, consider the inherent tension between liberty and discipline, individualism and the common good, authority and autonomy, revolution and preservation, equity and excellence, and the list goes on. For too long we have misunderstood this inherent tension within education and have turned competing social values into conflicts. Any one who has attended a school board meeting, lunched in a faculty lounge, or sat in faculty meetings knows of what I speak. Unfortunately, without understanding the role of tension, educators, parents, administrators will place themselves in certain camps, and the issue gets lost in an "us" against "them" fight. What is more productive is to articulate the issue as one of competing tensions that when explicated can be negotiated. We can learn to understand that the point of view of the "loyal opposition" is most likely based within a deeply held social value, rather than attributing their position to stupidity, stubbornness, laziness, or a multitude of other character defects. Rather than abhor or avoid another conflict, we can celebrate our ability to find a workable balance in a given paradox for our specific educational contexts. To undertake this complex task requires a willingness to construct a learning community built on trust, risk-taking, and good will, along with a healthy dose of humility. (I am sure that my words belie the difficulty of this task.)

Let me explain how it is helpful to educational dialogue to reframe our conflicts as tensions. Generally speaking, tension often is misunderstood in a negative light, for example, "tension in the air," or "tension headache," or the tension of a "fight brewing." Yet seen in a different light, tension, understood as a characteristic of "paradox in productive equilibrium," is a powerfully productive force.[9] Consider this. Tension can be understood as that which actually animates and brings life to a given endeavor. I take my examples from the world of art, music, and drama. I often ask my students who are artists and musicians to describe what role tension plays in their work. They tell me it is a critical part of their work that represents two competing tendencies trying to seek resolution, but never completely giving way to the other. They describe it as what gives energy to a piece of music or art. It is often the ability to capture and express this tension that differentiates a great piece of art from merely a competent one. Art without tension is boring. Surely it may entertain for a time, but it does not capture our imaginations or hearts, nor does it endure. To illustrate, I draw another example, this time from architecture. Think of the amazing engineering creation we know as the arch and the role of its keystone. The keystone functions as both the site and the mediator of tension. There are two exerting forces, which the keystone balances while redistributing the energy to hold the arch rather than let it destruct to the stronger of one side or the other.

Seen in this way, tension is a state that is necessary for an activity to be dynamic. We would hope education could be cast as such. It should not be a goal in education to resolve tension. Rather, it is important to understand its role, identify the social values at stake, and find a mediating balance point in what remains as intractable dilemmas. Recast as a positive and creative force, tension should be considered fluid and movable and should be valued as that which animates the moral dimensions of education.

By raising these issues, by seeing this work as a comment on the moral nature of education, by bringing an interdisciplinary lens to the discussion, by understanding the difference between conflict and tension, I hope that this work can inform the dialogue of educational reform. As educators, we share an underlying commitment to the well-being or flourishing of children's lives. We are concerned that many children are marginalized in the process of education, that many children fail to gain skills for leading full lives. We should even be concerned that most children find school boring! Just as important, we need to understand what occurs in those classrooms inhabited by children and *masterful* teachers. In order to do this, I argue that the notion of dignity is a crucial component of educational reform discourse and that it is generally not found in such dialogue. Instead, "best practices" or sweeping answers to our perceived educational problems are encapsulated by politicians in programs of "legislated excellence."[10] I claim that along with such research and policy, but prior to and foundational to it, must be a concern with the moral character of the relationships that occur at school. Without such a concern, researchers, whether they utilize complex statistical analyses or long-term ethnographies, will fail to reach the heart of the matter.

To illustrate, consider this example. Several years ago, Shirley Brice Heath visited the University of Washington and gave a thought-provoking lecture regarding her research work with drama and at-risk urban youth. She spoke of a powerful after-school theater program for inner-city at-risk children with whom she was involved. She described the hard work of those involved in these programs and the way that the children and adolescents would engage and sometimes be transformed by their involvement. Her work sounded wonderful! During the question and answer period following the lecture, a woman from the audience commented something to this effect: "Your after-school theater program sounds so marvelous. How can we transfer such a program into the public schools?"

While the question may sound benign, it illuminates the underlying assumption that we can simply transfer work from one domain to another. It betrays the complexity of the human relationships involved in this work. In our well-intentioned efforts to improve education for children, programs are often lifted like templates to be placed in another context. It is mistakenly thought that it is the program that solves the pressing problem. Missed is an acknowledgment of human needs such as recognition, trust, yearning, and community. Fundamentally, it is the character of the moral relationships that occur within these unique and special programs that address these needs. Innovative programs are necessary, but in exploring such programs, we cannot forget that at their foundation there must be a concern for the moral character of human relationships and needs. This is the point that I make herein.

To support the claims found within this work, I undertake a normative analysis. To describe the standpoint from which I undertake this work, it might be helpful to contrast the method I have chosen with other methods often used in educational research in order to highlight the differences. (My oversimplification of research methods here is meant to be illustrative only of pertinent differences and not the deep-seated epistemological issues existing between methods of inquiry!) One way to support a claim is by empirical evidence. Whether one is conducting an experiment or taking field notes, the justification supporting the research claim comes from empirical evidence. For example, in a quantitative analysis, one may manipulate variables and record what occurs thereafter, and through statistical analysis determine the extent of the variable's impact on a given event. Or by way of qualitative study, one may spend a good amount of time observing a particular event or particular events, becoming part of the process in question, and then generate descriptive or explanatory themes. Such analyses can be very complex. While important methods for garnering and analyzing data, these are not the methods I employ.

Another form of evidence employed to support a research claim is generated from an analytical philosophical method. This can be in the form of a tight argument (for example, in a syllogistic form), or by way of a conceptual analysis wherein one takes one or two related concepts and in a very detailed and methodical manner explicates a concept by indicating what it is and what it is not. For example, one could analyze what it means to be a person by examining in an abstract sense, the metaphysical nature of personhood. All this could be accomplished through conceptual analytic analysis without ever addressing the messiness, complexity, and contradictory nature of the human condition. While an appropriate and fruitful endeavor along one line of explanation, this is also not the method I employ.

The method I employ in order to generate my normative claims is one of laying out the best evidence for my claim. This evidence is drawn from various sources, including reasoned argument, broad conceptual analysis, case examples from schooling, stories from literature, and interpretation of the meaning of examples given. In addition, I draw upon the analyses of others as a part of building support for my normative claims. By drawing upon these sources, I employ a phenomenological approach. In other words, my claims are based upon how schooling is experienced by many. The type of "meaning" I am attempting to articulate herein is how the phenomena of schooling, education, and the associated relationships are experienced by the individuals involved. This is a different sense of meaning than that of the analytic philosopher who is aiming at a clear, intellectual, conceptual analysis. This method is similar to that employed in a court of law where the method is to garner the best evidence from various sources in order to make the strongest case possible.

In *The Uses of Argument*, Stephen Toulmin describes two models that can be used to support a claim. One is the logico-mathematical model, which is based on deductive reasoning from premises to conclusion. The other model to which Toulmin refers is jurisprudential. He indicates that such a model marshals evidence from various sources. For example, he indicates that the following activities are important to making a strong case: evidence regarding identification, testimony regarding an event, interpretation of statutes, claims for exemption from law, pleas for extenuation, and that which must be considered in coming to verdict and sentencing. For claims made in other arenas of inquiry, Toulmin argues that similar reasoning, drawn from multiple sources, must occur in order to take into account the complexity of the human situation. He states:

> When we turn from the special case of the law to consider rational arguments in general, we are faced at once by the question whether these must not be analysed [sic] in terms of an equally complex set of categories. If we are to set our arguments out with complete logical candor, and understand properly the nature of the "logical process," surely we shall need to employ a pattern of argument no less sophisticated than is required in the law.[11]

In writing this book, I have drawn upon multiple sources of evidence suggested by the jurisprudential model.

This method is eclectic in that it employs various strategies. Part of the conceptual analysis follows Green's process as noted earlier wherein one closely examines the ordinary concepts employed in support of education. Green notes:

> When we note the ordinary language of such common affairs, and the integument of logic by which these words are bound together or forever set apart, then the underlying structure of

our lives reveals itself. Habit is unwrapped; the concealed ethic, the ordinary is revealed. And in this unwrapping, the ordinary may appear as a fresh discovery even though there is nothing in it we did not already know. The ordinary unwrapped can surprise us. The medium of our thought—these ordinary words— can become the object of our thought, and when that happens, then philosophy has entered, not as someone else's text, but as our own. Philosophy appears as the logic of our common life.[12]

When I examine the concept of dignity or the concept of story, I am beginning with concepts that we employ in everyday life. We think we understand them and their place in our language and practice. By explicating them in the way Green describes, I uncover linkages between them and the process of education that may be unseen or unexamined. This type of analysis consequently generates my normative claims.

In addition, prior work in moral philosophy has explicated an important distinction that is useful to me. This distinction indicates that normative "ought" or "should" claims are sometimes inherent in the description of a concept. In this regard, John Searle argues against Hume who states that one cannot derive an "ought" from an "is." In his article "How to Derive 'Ought' from 'Is,'" Searle indicates that "ought" can be derived from "is" because "institutional facts exist within systems of constitutive rules."[13] It is the system of constitutive rules that gives meaning to a particular concept. Searle states that "some systems of constitutive rules involve obligations, commitments, and responsibilities. Within those systems we can derive 'oughts' from 'is's.'"

Searle provides the following examples. In the sport of baseball, when an umpire calls the base runner "out," he is implying a set of actions that must also take place beyond the description of his judgment that the ball reached second base before the runner. He is implying that the runner must now leave the field, that an "out" be charged against the at-bat team. What the player ought to do by virtue of being called "out" is derived from a certain set of constitutive rules that define the game of baseball. In another example regarding the meaning of debt, Searle states that "to recognize something as a debt is necessarily to recognize an obligation to pay it." Within the description of what the concept of debt means, lies the obligation of the debtor to pay. In like manner, inherent in the practice of education are certain oughts or shoulds. These constitutive rules often remain invisible and hidden. Yet they are consequential to the quality of the educative experience. Education proceeds by virtue of certain constitutive rules. In analyzing what education or dignity is, normative claims are generated regarding what we ought to do by virtue of being educators or sustaining dignity. This book addresses the oughts inherent in the concepts of education and dignity and points to some unexamined questions that might be asked of the constitutive rules of education.

Such is the nature of the contribution I hope to make in this book, employing the method that I have. Like Walker Percy, quoted in the excerpt at the beginning of this chapter, I am interested in bridging the gap between theory and practice, in addressing what our experience in education means, and in finding ways to "live out the rest of the day."

2

NO SMALL MATTER:

Dignity in the Context of Education

When it comes to education, we are bewildered! Many voices purport to tell us what is wrong with schools today. American education has been criticized for not meeting the needs of various constituencies, whether those needs are expressed as political or religious expectations, parent concerns, or student interests.[1] Communities, parents, and educational experts have addressed this problem, and many have worked long and hard to improve schools. Still we struggle. *Violence grows:* A student is shot dead standing outside her high school.[2] *Apathy increases:* A news writer reports that "Johnny can't read. He can't spell, either. He can't do basic math, and he doesn't know where Chile is or who was president before Reagan. What's worse, he doesn't care that he doesn't know."[3] *Marginalization continues:* For all the efforts of concerned persons, achievement and test scores of young black Americans lag far behind those of white Americans.[4]

Most would agree that the issues schools face are complex problems spawned by multiple social sources. Yet at the same time that we acknowledge the complexity of the problems made manifest in our schools, many of us still expect schools to provide a solution for the

problems that grow out of troubles in the community, the home, and
the nation. School represents the site of a tension between cause and
solution. On the one hand, it is acknowledged that the problems
that are manifest in schools today are created by a host of social
causes quite separate from the schools themselves; on the other hand,
schools are viewed as the site for remedying many of these problems.[5] Some have argued that placing the burden on schools to
address these social problems simply prevents us from having to do
larger and harder work, that is, remedy the larger social causes.[6] But
the feeling that we must *do* something remains. To complicate matters even more, there is some evidence that our schools actually *are*
better and the efforts put towards improving education are not
misplaced.[7] Still our bewilderment is manifest by the continuing sense
of unease with our schools, which is made explicit by educational
research, reform attempts, and media accounts. Thus, persons concerned with education respond: state mandated standards are added,
new pedagogical techniques are emphasized, revised curricula are
adopted, metal detectors are added at the doors to our schools.

But is it possible that we are asking the wrong questions and
looking in the wrong places? In efforts to reform education, many of
our appeals are not to what is truly educative, but to what is auxiliary
to education. Much of reform policy and research data apply to
things such as vocational preparedness, classroom management, cost
effectiveness, technology implementation, modes of assessment, and
equal opportunity. Far less of our attention is directed to investigat-
ing what is truly educative or to holding dialogue about educational
goods and values themselves.[8] Consider this example. Many times
the justification for a particular educational practice is that it will
prepare children for some experience coming in their future, usually a year or two away. So the typical turn in fifth grade to more
traditional academics is said to be necessary in order to prepare
children for the independence of middle school. In middle school,
more homework is given, fifty-minute class periods, and assignments
to multiple teachers are implemented in order to prepare students
for high school. In high school, tougher standards and tracking to
vocational or college courses are to prepare one for the rigors of
college, for the job world, for the S.A.T.s, or for . . . one need only fill
in the blank. In contrast to these instrumental needs, how often do
we ground our educational practices by an appeal based on truly
educative grounds? For example, if we were concerned with inquiry

regarding truly educative goods, we might spend more time asking, what does it look like to learn? What are components of education? How can we ensure that all children learn well? What are truly educative goods? More specifically, what is the value of reading a novel? Music and art education? A liberal arts course of study? Is the only measure of these values related to the preparation of the child for some distant future, to potential income earnings? Are there important educative goods that cannot be demonstrated by standardized measures of student performance? Or is there an educative value that cannot be quantified? In this regard, Alfie Kohn reminds us, "Apart from the skills that will be useful for students to have in the future, they ought to have a chance to choose in the present. Children, after all, are not just adults-in-the-making. They are people whose current needs and rights and experiences must be taken seriously."[9] So paying attention to the educative experiences of children while they are children is integral to improving education. I will argue that one of the primary goods in the education of children is dignity, and additionally that dignity should play a foundational role in determining the character of education. It is to this that my book speaks. Through this chapter, I describe the broad claims I will make in order to provide an overall framework for understanding the intent of this work. The chapters following will then provide an analysis of the concepts and relationships I posit herein.

I begin by turning our attention to the notion of dignity and its place in our schools. Taking a closer look in the schools, we will find an abrogation given little attention in the media blitz on education. We find the abrogation of dignity. In many places, certainly not just in the school alone, the fundamental dignity of the children in our midst is ignored. Lacking quantifiable measures, we pay little attention to the topic. But being fundamental to the task of education, dignity is important in any talk of what it means to educate.

Too often the notion of dignity may become confused with notions of loving one's students or building self-esteem or in senses of caring that are mistakenly diluted as soft and mushy goals. This is not the sense of dignity that I employ here. Mine is not a psychological sense, but is situated in the moral domain of our relationships. In fact, it is instantiated in the space of relationship. It is what I acknowledge by virtue of our common humanity and what makes moral demands upon me regarding my treatment of you. In the not-quite-public, not-quite-private world of school, I would prefer that

teachers display a commitment to the *dignity* of all their students
rather than a commitment to *love* all their students. We all know that
you cannot really love them all to the same degree. There are those
few special teachers with whom I made a deep connection throughout my educational life and others with whom my friends connected.
To seek this same level of connection with every teacher and child
would lessen the unique quality of love or friendship that makes it
powerful in the first place. Conversely, dignity, by its very definition,
extends to all and can be so realized without compromising the
nature of the idea itself.

Understanding the vital role of dignity in education is crucial
because the consequence of this abrogation of our children's dignity
is their marginalization. As described in *Savage Inequalities,* the consequences of marginalization are overwhelmingly apparent in dilapi-
dated schools where children study amidst toxic hazards, in cold and
drafty buildings and with few and shabby supplies.[10] While Kozol's
books paint a morally abhorrent picture of the conditions in which
we require our children to be educated, it is the immediacy of the
human voice we dare not ignore. In "Children in America's Schools,"
a recent Bill Moyer special on the state of equitable funding in
education, a young adolescent girl from a poor, white, rural school
poignantly asks the adversarial and powerful adults arguing about
equitable education, "Look me in the eye and tell me that I'm not
worth it (the money required for equal funding)."[11] But marginalization also exists where children sit comfortably in suburban
school settings or in privileged private schools.[12] Children of diverse
economic and ethnic backgrounds often are made to feel as if they
do not belong in schools. As noted earlier, all we have to do is listen
carefully to many adolescents: "School is boring." "School feels like
a prison." "No one knows me here." "I don't care about grades." We
have all heard this disturbing lack of engagement so often that we
often dismiss this attitude as normal. In writing this book, I hope to
address the complexity and character of both the apparent and the
hidden types of marginalization in order to challenge the normalcy
of these disengaged attitudes toward schooling.[13]

Generally speaking, marginalization denotes a pushing to the
periphery or margins; not including as central to a given endeavor.
This pushing to the margins can occur in various ways: physical,
psychological, intellectual, moral, or any combination of these. When
one speaks of marginalization, one also conjures up images of invis-

ibility and powerlessness. But in education, it is absurd to countenance the marginalization of children since the very task of education is to teach children, and hence one would assume that they would be at the center of this process. How could children be on the margins of such an endeavor or not central to the task? If marginalization occurs in schools, miseducation is taking place. It is safe to say that education that marginalizes is an oxymoron. Although it is incongruent with the idea of education, children *are* marginalized in schools. The marginalization I will speak of occurs throughout the daily relationships between adults and children at school. Most times it is not glaring; it is subtle.

Although I will discuss marginalization more fully in chapter 3, I present my argument, in brief, here: One debilitating way that children are marginalized in schools is along lines of their differences, such as race, class, gender, and disability. I call this "stereotypic marginalization." In addition, children are also marginalized in schools in a manner that may encompass but can go beyond these traditional classifications of difference. This second type of marginalization (which is of primary interest in this book), occurs in the realm of personal identity and meaning for the developing child. I call this "psycho-social marginalization." This is not to say that stereotypic marginalization does not profoundly affect personal identity. Nor is it to say that stereotypic marginalization does not carry grave consequences. But it is possible to imagine persons who are marginalized based on their difference, yet who still have a strong sense of self generated from their own family and/or community. Hence, while stereotypic marginalization would be harmful in other ways to such persons, their identity making may not necessarily be severely impacted. Both types of marginalization are interactive and often occur together, but it is important to make a distinction between the two forms so the often overlooked psycho-social marginalization can be made manifest and addressed. By confounding the two, we miss seeing the pervasiveness of the "psycho-social marginalization" in schools and the need for it to be challenged. Unfortunately, if we cast marginalization only as an issue based on race, class, and gender, then it allows too many of us to turn away from the problem by attributing it to the "other." We can say, "This is not my problem," "This is not my school," "This is not my child." Hence, to avoid the slip in our moral obligation to all children, this book examines what may appear as subtle forms of marginalization and assaults on the dignity of all our children. Following Green's advice to "unwrap the ordinary" and make "evident what we already know, but may have overlooked," we may see that the ordinary is not so subtle at all.

While psycho-social marginalization is destructive of personal identity and meaning, hence an affront to dignity, paying attention to the meaning persons are attempting to make in their lives enhances identity and a sense of dignity. Given the central tasks of development, I will argue that paying attention to what I will call "core stories" is the way to understand the meaning children are creating in their lives. Therefore, in order to sustain dignity and overcome marginalization, schools should pay attention to the stories children are making, that is, the sense and meaning they are trying to make of their lives. To do less is to abrogate the dignity of our young, and thus, to miseducate.

To illustrate how this might occur, I offer these small cases. I caution that these examples are not meant to be unduly critical or prescriptive. They are offered as illustrations of what often goes on in a typical school day. The intent of my investigation is to ask us to stop and examine what may be the unintended consequences of how we practice education. Only when we have brought such an examination to our practice and its consequences can we be more confident that our practice reflects our commitments. Consider these examples gleaned from observations at schools.

Jane rushes in from recess to tell her teacher how a fellow student shoved her on the playground and she fell and hurt herself. Seeing no blood, the teacher gestures with her hand to stop the tale and reminds the little girl that it is the classroom rule that no tattling is allowed when coming in from recess. After all, the teacher was not there to see what happened. How could she take sides? She ushers Jane into the classroom since she was holding up the rest of the children from coming in and getting settled for afternoon activities.

Surely this is a familiar occurrence to anyone involved in elementary education. But stop for a moment and ask, What is the meaning that Jane is trying to communicate to her teacher? Jane was shoved and hurt at recess. She is attempting to gain an acknowledgment of that hurt, physical and emotional, as well as an acknowledgment that she matters more than the rule about not tattling. Who is willing to give this kind of attention? And what are the costs of not paying attention to this meaning? Classroom efficiency may be gained, but at what cost to the child who is asking for an acknowledgment that she matters? Of course, acknowledgment alone is rarely enough to enhance dignity, but it certainly is where a teacher should start when concerned with paying attention to the meaning in children's lives.

Samuel is a very bright child who comes into his second-grade classroom full of knowledge about his world. His parents have made it a priority to enrich the lives of their children. But Samuel quickly gets lost in the classroom because he is rather shy and well behaved. A unit on whales piques Samuel's interest and rather uncharacteristically he gregariously shares his "extra" knowledge of whales. "Oh my! Samuel," said his teacher, "you know so much about whales! But we have to move on now." And she begins to read the class a story. Samuel sits down. The teacher never remembers to ask Samuel about whales, and he ventures nothing further.

The meaning Samuel is attempting to convey is slightly different from that of Jane. Here is a case where he, as a meaning maker, is entirely overlooked as the teacher unloads the curriculum on him and the other children, rather than knowing who each child is and building curriculum and pedagogy upon that knowledge. Samuel, as a person, is made invisible. The curriculum dominates his school life. The curriculum is what takes center stage. It is what matters. Hence, prioritizing curriculum leads Ira Shor to comment that with the traditional syllabus, most students feel that education is "something done to them, not something they do."[14] If the notion of dignity is to be foundational in our educational practice, then we must examine how curriculum can enrich a student-centered pedagogy, rather than dominate it.

A fourth-grade teacher stands in front of her class one month into the school year. "Today I've divided the class into teams. Each group has a team leader appointed. We will change team members throughout the year, but the team leaders will remain. Some children have talent at one thing such as sports or spelling, and other children have talent at being leaders. Those children I've seen with leadership qualities have been appointed your leaders for the year. Every Friday we will have silent lunch, so the team leaders and I can meet and discuss problems in the groups during that time." How many children are in the class? Twenty-eight. How many leaders does this teacher acknowledge among those fourth-grade children? Six.

What makes us feel uncomfortable with this teacher's attribution of leadership talent to only six children in her class? Perhaps it is the implicit assumption that leadership is either present or not at the tender age of nine or ten. Yet how can this be congruent with a notion of education that, by its very definition, assumes there is room for growth and development? What room is there for meaning to grow? If leadership ability is already determined to be present or absent at nine years of age, what implications are there for any other types of meaning that children could develop?

Latisha rushed into the school office at the beginning of lunch recess. Her teacher was already in the faculty room, and Latisha was just reminded by another student that she was to attend the Student Council meeting during lunch. Not knowing where the meeting was to be held, she went into the office, but made one vital mistake. She did not have a pass from her teacher. She opened her mouth to ask the secretary where the Student Council meeting was being held, and before she could get more than a word or two out, the secretary held up her hand and said, "Stop! Latisha, you don't have a pass, so you have no business being in the office. You know the rules. I can't talk to you," and she turned and walked away. Latisha, fighting back tears of embarrassment and disappointment, left the office and after recess had to explain to her teacher why she did not represent her class at the Student Council meeting.

In this example, Latisha's meaning (and attendant enthusiasm) was dominated by an adult who imposed her story, a story of rules, onto the child. Latisha was willing to engage in the activities of the school, thereby furthering that elusive "learning community" we strive to create. She went to those adults who are charged with the care of children. Yet she never was given the chance to even explain the purpose of her visit to the office. She never had a chance to be heard. Only one meaning was allowed: the meaning of the rules as understood by the school secretary.

Surrounded by anxious and excited twelve and thirteen year olds and their parents, I attended an orientation to middle school. Hoping I would hear about the faculty's commitment to learning, to children, to diversity, I was disappointed that almost the entire hour was taken up by a monologue about school rules. Some might say my disappointment is a little thing. But I ask you to put yourself in the place of one of the young students who sat around me. Excited and scared at the same time, they are growing up and entering a distinctively different type of school experience from what they experienced in elementary school. Here they will have six or seven teachers instead of one; they will have a locker; they will have school dances; they wonder whether they will be liked, whether they can do the school work, whether they'll make the basketball team. Amidst the jumble of all these anticipatory feelings, they receive a litany of rules: "Welcome to the middle school. We're excited you're here. So we can all have a great experience here, let me tell you the rules." And then the list begins. Is it any wonder that kids soon begin to fidget and their eyes wander? What an opportunity was missed to engage these students and their equally anxious parents with a discussion and illustration of the great commitment to children learning and growing. Certainly, rules have a part of every social situation and institution within which we live. This inquiry is asking us to consider what message our children receive and internalize about their education when the adults entrusted with their care prioritize the rules of the school over the growth and development of the children. What an opportunity is missed to include the incoming parents and students in developing their school rules!

Of what are these cases instances? Poor teaching? Misguided staff? Isolated bad judgment? Some would even argue that they represent best practices since surely the teacher can not handle all the individual requests and needs made by students each day, or as I have heard my own students tell me, "That's just the way things are." But something more fundamental is occurring here. These instances represent a lack of paying attention to the meaning that children are creating in their lives. They represent a lack of paying attention to the dignity of the child who is attempting to communicate to a significant other in her life, "I matter." What is deeply troubling is that in each of these instances, the children engaged an adult entrusted with their care, whether they were making a request, offering a comment, or attending a school meeting. These educators were teaching school. They were teaching a class. They were teaching a curriculum. But they were not teaching children because they were not paying attention to the meaning that each child brings with him or herself and is in the process of making. In ignoring the meaning the child is attempting to share, they diminish the dignity of the child in each case. Do I believe that this was the intent of these educators? Absolutely not, but without the type of inclusive moral dialogue I am advocating here, the unintended consequences of not paying attention to children occurs.

What is this connection between meaning and dignity? Dignity consists in recognizing the right to create one's own original life. (This right resides in the realm of the moral, rather than the legal.) It involves the process of humanization, or in other words, what we do by virtue of being human. The parameters that surround how one goes about such a task, the role of the self and authorship in the creation of one's life, and the focus on the importance of defining the task of creating one's life are influenced by the cultures within which we are each situated. Such a task is always dialogical—never accomplished in isolation, but in relation with others. As we are immersed in social relations throughout our lives, we are necessarily creating meaning. When I speak of meaning, I intend the word to convey one's attempt at making sense of life experience. One definition of "meaning" in the *Oxford English Dictionary* speaks to the understanding I employ here. It defines meaning as "the signification, sense, import; a sense, interpretation. Also, the intent, spirit as apart from the 'letter' (of a statement, law, etc.)." Here meaning carries with it a sense of personal or subjective interpretation and import. It is the significance or import underlying our everyday activities and narrative. In turn, this making sense contributes to the ability to create a sense of a coherence or identity.

Dignity affirms identity and meaning as it privileges the life-building process. Identity and meaning are related to each other in the following way. They stand in a symbiotic relationship. While always in development, identity is less fluid than meaning, though never fixed. Identity represents the very personal "who I am." However, meaning speaks to what sense I make of my experience. This sense or meaning I am making contributes to how I define myself, that is, my identity. Identity involves seeking a more or less coherent sense of self, while meaning making is the process that leads to the development of such an identity at any given time. The distinction is subtle, but important. Because the two realms are distinct, an individual has room to create meaning before it is incorporated into identity. As I will discuss in chapter 5, this "play or wiggle" space between identity and meaning is part of the role for narrative or story. In this way, both identity and meaning making are interactively constitutive of the self. Being constitutive of the self (i.e., the creation of one's life), dignity's role is to sustain and enhance the self engaged in these processes.

Attention to dignity must represent more than a demand to be left alone, though, at times, such a demand is appropriate. Paying attention to dignity must incorporate a relational and proactive sense of creating a life, because one cannot create a life in any other manner. A life cannot be created in isolation. While we all have varying degrees of engagement with our social world, it is impossible to imagine a young child left entirely on his or her own to create a life. This would not be sustaining the dignity of the child. It would

be abusive neglect. Therefore, because it is the case that creating a
life entails proactive social engagement in order to create meaning,
dignity requires sustaining such endeavors. Regarding this point,
Jerome Bruner explains how individual development is strongly influenced by the cultural milieu into which a child is born. But this
is just a beginning. By virtue of being a participant in a given culture,
and by virtue of the processes of shared meaning development, the
individual both shapes and is shaped by the communal experience.
Bruner states:

> Given that psychology is so immersed in culture, it must be or-
> ganized around those meaning-making and meaning-using pro-
> cesses that connect man to culture. This does not commit us to
> more subjectivity in psychology; it is just the reverse. By virtue of
> participation in culture, meaning is rendered public and shared.
> Our culturally adapted way of life depends upon shared mean-
> ings and shared concepts and depends as well upon shared modes
> of discourse of negotiating differences in meaning and interpre-
> tation. The child does not enter the life of his or her group as
> a private and autistic sport of primary processes, but rather as a
> participant in a larger public process in which public meanings
> are negotiated.[15]

Because this essence of being human, the project of self-creation is
a socially-dependent one, it becomes a project of which education
must take account. As educators, we must acknowledge and create
the shared space for such cultural meanings to be explored and
negotiated. The development of the self requires this communal
dimension.

At this point, it would be helpful to make a comment about the
conceptualization of sustaining dignity. One might think that all that
is entailed in sustaining dignity is to support it when one recognizes
it. But phrases such as *preserving* or *sustaining* dignity could be considered "formaldehyde language," for example, that one possesses
dignity and it only needs to be preserved, similar to the way one
preserves a lab frog! This certainly is not the usage intended here.
Sustaining dignity would include all those social activities and attitudes needed to develop, pay attention to, and create an environment for the dignity of children to flourish. This more fully explicated
notion of sustaining dignity is elaborated in chapter 4 and represents
an active, rich, and social sense of dignity.

Because schools have been given the moral obligation to care for children and their development, schools must be concerned with the dignity of their students and must do so in a way that goes beyond lip-service notions of dignity in codes of ethics or mission statements. Education requires paying attention to the creation of identity and meaning, and not just the typical educational task of "learning the curriculum." These two tasks cannot be divorced from one another as we are often prone to do when discussing educational purposes.

If schools are to pay attention to the creation and development of children's lives, then paying attention to the dignity of children should be the foundational task of schools. (This claim will be further elaborated in chapter 4.) Historically, there has always been much contention about the purposes of schooling. Joel Spring identifies three comprehensive purposes of schooling.[16] They are the political, the social and the economic. The political purpose includes preparing students for democratic citizenship. The social purpose includes all that goes into maintaining social control and creating social conditions that are conducive to community or civic life. Finally, the economic purpose speaks to what is necessary for the continued development of national wealth, a prepared labor force, and world-class technology. These purposes presuppose that education's role can be reduced to preparing students to meet any or all of these missions. Of course, emphases vary and purposes are articulated and embellished in each generation. But any of these purposes assumes a child prepared to learn. In other words, there must be selves to pursue these (or other) purposes. While there are many purposes of schooling, without paying attention to the identity development and meaning making of the child, there would be no constituted self to educate. In this way, paying attention to the dignity of the child is foundational to the purposes of education.

Some might say that surely the school cannot be responsible for all the developmental needs of the child. I would agree that the primary responsibility for childhood growth and development lies with the family, and more generally, the "village," but because children do not set their developmental tasks aside or check them at the door of the classroom, or hang them in the locker with their coats, schools also become responsible for paying attention to the creation of a life. Certainly there are many things that a child must have in order to develop well, and most would agree that the school cannot do it all, nor should it. For example, how much health care, psychological services, clothing, or food should a school provide?[17] While answers to these questions vary by school and community, these services are significantly different from paying attention to the place of dignity in schools. Although children require all the above to lead happy, healthy lives, every school population varies in its needs and in its resources to provide such services.

Dignity, as instantiated in the quality of moral relationships that occur in schools, must be provided for all children regardless of socio-economic class or other factors. For the same reason that dignity is foundational to any other purpose of school—that is, it is the process wherein selves are constituted—so the sustaining of dignity trumps other claims for goods and services. Dignity provides the room for persons to create their lives as narratives. Schools are places where children spend significant hours of their lives. Considering that children are developing in so many ways and creating their lives, sustaining dignity means more than simply standing by and admiring them. To varying degrees, it means assisting children in creating their own lives. Some children come to us with rich and full selves, while others come thin and fragile. Sustaining dignity, in a proactive way, would be concerned with the flourishing of children's lives in whatever condition they come.

When I claim that a concern for dignity should be foundational to the tasks of school, I do not mean that identity making is the focal task of schools in that the bulk of time spent on tasks should explicitly revolve around this. I do not mean that it is exclusive of other tasks or educational goods. I do mean that sustaining dignity by paying attention to identity and meaning for the developing child should be conceived as a basic purpose when answering questions such as Why am I teaching this? Why does our school do it this way and not another? What is the story of this child and how does it fit into her or his learning here? How can we help this child succeed? In other words, a concern for dignity is foundational to our subsequent educational decisions. Without it, education is lacking, because it neglects the constitutive development of the self in both its personal and social forms. The concern for dignity must be one that directs the activities of the teacher and the school. Additionally, the concern for the dignity of children should become a cogent part of the discussions of those involved in school reform efforts today. In other words, it must orient the dialogues of educators, academics, researchers, and parents as they map out curriculum, methodology, and the character of the classroom and school itself.

In order to sustain dignity in this proactive sense, schools must pay attention to creating a context where identities can be nurtured and where the development and articulation of meaning is honored. Story is a vehicle for such an endeavor, and I will explicate its role in chapter 5. But I would like to make a preliminary distinction. Throughout this book I utilize the notion of core stories, as distinct from that of a traditional story format. This distinction has broad implications for schooling. For example, while others rightly have worked to include diverse historical, cultural, and autobiographical stories in the content of schooling, my notion of core stories speaks to a moral understanding of how we give and receive meaning and how the preservation of dignity must be of paramount concern to educators seeking to overcome the marginalization that occurs in schools.[18] The role I posit for paying attention to core stories is prior to and foundational to work in curriculum, pedagogy, and policy. Understanding the notion of core stories means understanding that story is the narrative carrier of meaning, both individually and culturally. Therefore, paying attention to stories has implications not only for marginalization based on race, class, and gender, but for the deeper notion of psycho-social marginalization that affects the development of the self for many students in our schools today. The contribution of this work is to examine the particular role that core stories, as carriers of meaning, play within education and how that relates to dignity.

I argue that paying attention to the notion of core stories is a necessary (although not sufficient) condition to overcome this marginalization, because of the unique characteristics of story that will be discussed in a later chapter. I do not make the claim that understanding the fundamental role of dignity will solve the educational conundrum, but I do maintain that without understanding the fundamental role of dignity in education, the multifaceted educational reforms we conspire to enact will be ineffective. This is so because psycho-social marginalization puts our children's dignity, and thus their very selves, at risk.

One last point. I must ask myself, who would argue with the idea that schools should sustain the dignity of the child? After all, such a commitment is already found in educators' professional documents, such as the following: "The educator, believing in the worth and dignity of each human being, recognizes the supreme importance of the pursuit of truth, devotion to excellence, and the nurture of democratic principles."[19] So if it seems self-evident that such a claim is noncontroversial, then what is the purpose of my writing? I suggest that while the word *dignity* may be invoked on behalf of children on some occasions, we do not understand the following about our invocation. First, we do not understand the depth and importance of making dignity a fundamental and real concern of schools. Hence, we should ask, What would education look like that took seriously the claim that we must pay attention to the dignity of the child? Second, even if we accept dignity as a legitimate concern for educators, we do not clearly understand the link between our actions and decisions as educators and the dignity of the child. Third, in accepting dignity as a foundational concern for schools, we also must understand the fine distinctions between purported ways of sustaining dignity that may actually be dominating and abusive and those ways that truly sustain dignity and lead to the flourishing of children's lives.

This book examines these claims in more detail. To argue in support of the above, in chapter 3 I will lay out the problem of marginalization, in our schools, discussing the relationships among dignity, marginalization and resistance. In chapter 4, I will take an in-depth look at what dignity means in the context of education. This necessitates exploring the relationship between dignity and identity and introduces the idea that story is a vehicle for dignity. In addition, I will discuss how selves are construed in narrative terms and how this narrative nature of the self allows stories to carry meaning. Chapter 5 explicates the role and power of story in the development of identity and meaning, discussing the characteristics of story and how they allow story to be a vehicle for sustaining dignity. In chapter 6 I will explore the moral responsibilities attendant to the telling and hearing of core stories, including a discussion of how stories may be used for domination by others. Finally, in chapter 7 I discuss what it means to pay attention to stories in the context of education in order to overcome marginalization and nurture dignity in our children's lives.

A work of this sort carries a caveat. As I speak to the conditions of human life generally and, more specifically, the conditions under which we educate and care for children, the conceptual distinctions I attempt to make will of necessity be somewhat provisional. The complexity of any of the issues discussed here cannot adequately be represented by a series of chapters laid out in linear fashion. But, at the same time, in order to make a cogent contribution to a discussion of these issues, it is important to tease out distinctions, make clear relationships between concepts, and raise moral questions. Such is the character of this work. Therefore, while the reader will see a separate chapter on marginalization, a chapter on dignity, and then a chapter on stories, the reader should be aware that all of these concepts are intertwined in the lives of young people in schools. In like manner, I will address some themes as they cross these conceptual notions. For example, the theme of authenticity will appear related to several different concepts, such as authorship or listening, and the theme of narrative will be applied in several different contexts, such as marginalization and dignity. For purposes of this work, then, my discussion notes the complexity of the ideas presented, while at the same time attempting to address them clearly.

3

Ignoring the Demands of Dignity:
Marginalization and Resistance

The Nature of Marginalization

Schools are places where children spend more of their waking hours than anywhere else.[1] Because adults stand in a special moral relation to children and schools are where we find children, attention must be paid to the moral dimension of schooling. Therefore, adults in the schools should pay attention to the moral obligation of caring for children, with the understanding that the central task of the school is to educate children. Hence, education should occur with attention paid to the moral dimension of the relationships that occur within the educative process. One could posit an even stronger point: that paying attention to the moral obligation of caring for children is an essential part of education and to do otherwise would be to miseducate. In this regard, I call upon John Goodlad's definition of education wherein he states:

> Education, then, is a process of individual becoming. The aim of education is to have this process occur or, better, to have it flourish. The essence of the process is the growth taking place in the individual and the meaning of that growth for the individual. The richer that meaning, the more it creates a desire for

31

continued growth and the better the quality of the educational experience.[2]

Unfortunately, attention to the moral dimension of what occurs in schools is often lacking. In considering how to make schools more effective, little discussion is centered on the quality and character of the relationships that happen at school or on the nature of truly educative goods and values. Consequently, the experiences our children have in our schools are often morally harmful and unknown to us. I am not referring to those horribly abusive experiences perpetrated by adults with an intent to harm children, but I am talking about those experiences that may occur simply because we do not often stop and pay attention to the character and quality of the daily interactions that comprise what we call "education." It is not a new idea that schooling implies more than curricular content. Just as important, the notion of schooling implicates the structure, the standards, the governance, the financing, the multiple relationships that occur within a school day. Imagine for a moment the hallways of a secondary school during passing time, or the locker room during changing time, or the recess field. All of these aspects of schooling are educative or not, regardless of whether we adults are engaged in teaching. In any of these arenas, the environment for schooling that we create may not be truly educative, often because we have not wondered about the entire spectrum of the school day and measured it against the yardstick of being educative. One of the byproducts of this inattention to the moral and personal realm of education is marginalization.

Let us begin by looking more closely at the notion of marginalization. As described earlier and as the word implies, marginalization denotes a pushing to the periphery or margins. Utilizing this image, marginalization implies that there is a center or central part to any given activity, concern, or relationship, and being marginalized means not being included as central to a given endeavor. This pushing to the margins can occur in various realms of human activity: physical, psychological, intellectual, moral, or others. Consider these examples of marginalization: In the past those persons with physical handicaps often have been pushed to the margins of normal daily activity by the lack of access provided for their special needs. Historically, girls and women were considered too intellectually feeble to withstand the rigors of higher education and hence were not allowed to the center of advanced intellectual activity, such as, the university. In

Kohlberg's stages of moral development, girls often were seen as lacking higher-ordered moral reasoning skills, until Gilligan's work challenged the paradigm that privileged a singular way of understanding moral thought. In all these cases, there was some activity where individuals were not considered central to the task at hand and were dismissed to the edges of that activity. They were marginalized and as a result of that marginalization were unable to participate in and partake of the "promised goods" of that activity.

Now, recall that the moral imperative of dignity calls us to recognize others' rights to create their own original lives with their attendant identity development and meaning-making activities. We need then ask what marginalization would look like in the realms that are associated with creating a life.[3] As argued earlier, this notion of creating one's life is one of the moral components of education. If persons are pushed from the center to the margins of the activity of identity development and meaning making, then their dignity is diminished and marginalization has occurred in the following ways: the meaning one gives to one's life is ignored, one's meaning is dominated by others (in both the lives of the privileged as well as those oppressed), and requirements are made of one which are not relevant to one's life. The relevancy I speak of here is not that of momentary personal interest in a topic, but a relevance that must speak deeply to the projects of one's life making.

Speaking of education and relevancy, John Dewey describes the process as follows:

> The child's own instincts and powers furnish the material and give the starting-point for all education. Save as the efforts of the educator connect with some activity which the child is carrying on of his own initiative independent of the educator, *education becomes reduced to a pressure from without*. It may, indeed, give certain external results, but cannot truly be called educative.[4]

The marginalization that occurs from this type of external pressure damages dignity when efforts to educate do not connect with the meaning one is creating in one's life. In other words, education of this sort is not just pedagogically unsound, it lacks a moral nature as it marginalizes the self. In education of this ilk, someone else is trying to determine the meaning in a way that does not take into account the meaning life has for the particular individual. Rather, the educator concerned with Dewey's account of relevancy should be able to answer questions such as How does this connect to the child's life? What difference will this information make? Who knows what about this topic already? and What things really motivate learning in this particular child? These and similar questions forge the link between relevancy and education. This is a critical point to understand, because sometimes the two notions, growth and relevancy, may appear to be unrelated. Education necessarily means growth; this implies going beyond where one is at the moment.[5] Relevancy means having a concern for what is. A teacher's role is to take both into account. She must understand where the child is currently and use that as the background for where she envisions the student going. So one of the ways that children are marginalized in schools is when the meaning they give to their lives is peripheral to what is taught and how it is taught.

Herbert Kohl provides an example of just such a situation. He was invited to a school in San Antonio, Texas, that primarily served a Latino population. The school was struggling with academic success, and school officials asked Kohl to assist them in addressing issues related to student behavior and diversity. Students acted bored, uninterested, belligerent in classes. Kohl was asked to come and observe and provide suggestions for improvement. One day he visited a junior high history classroom where students were exhibiting thoroughly disengaged behaviors. After no one volunteered to read the textbook, *The First People to Settle Texas,* the teacher began reading himself. "The first people to settle Texas arrived from New England and the South in . . . " Kohl describes what happened next. "Two boys in the back put their hands in their eyes, there were a few giggles and some murmuring. One hand shot up, and that student blurted out, 'What are we, animals or something?' " The teacher gave up, introduced Kohl as a substitute teacher, and left the room. For a moment there was silence. Kohl reread the sentence and then asked the students whether they believed it. Kohl acknowledged that the textbook contained lies, and as he continued, students began to turn their attention to Kohl and the historical misrepresentation of history, a history they knew very well because it was part of their own cultural story. Needless to say, when Kohl invited these students to the dialogue by engaging in an honest discussion that acknowledged their lives, their culture, and their history, these heretofore belligerent, bored, restless, and disengaged students came to the educational table. As Kohl describes it:

The class launched into a serious and sophisticated discussion of the ways racism manifested itself in their everyday lives at school. And they described the stance they took in order to resist that racism and yet not be thrown out of school. It amounted to nothing less than full-blown, cooperative not-learning. They accepted the failing grades not-learning produced in exchange for the passive defense of their personal and cultural integrity.[6]

As the classroom culture made room for a more inclusive history to be told, these students were able to stretch beyond their dismissive attitudes because they and the wholeness of their lives were invited into the classroom. Prior to this, students were marginalized because what they were being taught had no connection to the cultural meaning that existed in their own daily lives. Not only was there no connection, but what the students were being taught was a negation of their own story.

Turning to an examination of the two types of marginalization described earlier—stereotypic and psycho-social—let me first note that it is important to make the distinction between these two types of marginalization because confusing them prevents us from seeing psycho-social marginalization, which is more subtle. When psycho-social marginalization is buried in the more typical discussion of stereotypic marginalization, we are prevented from addressing the issues necessary to its alleviation. Addressing marginalization at the psycho-social level is crucial to this discussion because if marginalization were only structurally induced, then institutional change would alleviate the problem in our attempts to address stereotypical marginalization. Yet many counter-examples abound. For instance, mandatory school bussing would have solved the issue of equity in education, but it did not. Remedial special education programs would have solved the issue of student achievement, but they did not. Two reasons why institutional change fails when it only makes structural changes are as follows. First, the institutional level does not necessarily address the complex dynamics of human interaction. The structure of the institution itself cannot be designed to take into account each possible human situation or for understanding varying human motivations. Second, educational policy traditionally frames the issue as one to be "solved." Such a preoccupation belies the complex, human interaction that occurs during schooling. It places its trust in the technocratic solution, that is, the confidence that we, using our rational minds and technological advances, can simply persist until we find the answer that works or solves the problem! Moreover, in defining the problem as one to be solved, we either ignore the developing self or utilize impoverished senses of the self and other. Discussions about resolving the complex social problems of marginalization must incorporate both the psycho-social and the stereotypic categories.[7] Before proceeding to the realm of the psycho-social, it is necessary to understand the role of the stereotypic and how that intersects with the psycho-social.

STEREOTYPIC MARGINALIZATION

Researchers, media reports, and personal experience have provided persuasive evidence of marginalization of students along lines of race, class, gender, and other predetermined differences, such as age or disability.[8] Many children of color and poor children face uphill battles when they come to school. Too often, children who live in poverty or who have different ethnicities have lower test scores, higher drop-out rates, and disproportionate special needs labeling and disciplinary actions in our public schools.[9] In other words, because of categorizable differences, these children face the possibility of being marginalized based on someone's stereotypic characterizations of their difference.

Patricia Hill Collins elucidates how marginalization occurs when the dominant culture sets up a subject-object dichotomy based on cultural classifications. According to Collins, "either/or dichotomous thinking categorizes people, things, and ideas in terms of their difference from one another."[10] In this model, difference is perceived as oppositional in nature. In other words, if you are not one way, then you are the other. There is no middle ground to see difference as existing in harmony or balance, rather than in opposition in an "either/or" sense. This creates educational settings where students are perceived as either good students or bad students, quiet and responsible students or obnoxious and irresponsible students. Our tendency to dichotomize students in this way prevents us from acknowledging the continuum of student behavior and its interactive relationship with culture and schooling.

In *Schooling Homeless Children*, Quint tells the story of how a teacher's response to a student was changed, not when the student's behavior changed, but when the teacher came to know the circumstances of the child's life experience. Six-year-old Jewel was disruptive in class, purposely knocking over chairs and books and responding to teachers with a declaration of, "Get outta my face." Intimidating and infuriating, to be sure, to a classroom teacher who was trying to teach all her students. With the encouragement of her principal, Jewel's teacher visited the homeless shelter where Jewel was staying with her mother. There she saw the "sad little faces and . . . scrawny little bodies huddled together," in their effort simply to survive the vicissitudes of life that they themselves never invited. After spending some time at the shelter and coming to understand this life context for her student, Jewel, the teacher remarked, "She has come a long way since I began to look at life from her point of view."[11] The important point of this story is that Jewel's teacher gave up a dichotomous framework in working with students. She knew that the behavior that was manifested was not all there was to this child, and it was not until she, as a teacher, understood that the disruptive behavior had a cause and was not simply rebellious obnoxiousness, that she could relate to Jewel in a new way that ultimately moderated Jewel's behavior in the classroom.

Those who are from groups traditionally oppressed often bear the brunt of more than one class of marginalization. They may face multiple marginalizations that occur when we do not bother to respond to the person as an individual, but respond only to the external differences we see. In this sense, individuals are symbolic representations of a category, constructed mainly, though not exclusively, by the dominant culture. I call marginalization based on these categories "stereotypic marginalization," for example, taking one set of characteristics and generalizing them to all persons possessing the observable difference. This results in shallow and usually erroneous characterizations about people. It is important to note that when this occurs, it is not about who *you* are as a person; it is about who *I* think you are. This is what characterizes the "subject-object" relationship, for example, "I am the subject, and you are the object whom I will define." It precludes your role in defining who you are.

Stereotypic marginalization often objectifies the person as the "other." Valerie Polakow notes that the terms *other* and *otherness* are often used when marginalizing persons based on these socially defined differences. This particular use of the term *other* denotes a dismissal of individuals and the meaning they attribute to their lives. Polakow describes this type of dismissal as follows: "The interpersonal distance and the alienation of self from other selves, the distancing of the individual from the human community, are underlying themes embodied in otherness. Otherness symbolizes the objectification-through-language and policy of those who are consigned to the margins of society."[12]

This description also sounds like the dichotomous subject-object distinction that Collins argues allows for the marginalization of others to occur. When one is made entirely into an other, marginalization becomes devastating in that such dismissal prohibits or discourages one from engaging in events, activities, or a community. If one cannot engage in a given endeavor, then one cannot profit from the experience. One cannot gain recognition, nor can one reap the advantages of participation, either the internal or external goods associated with a given endeavor. Such an individual becomes invisible because the dominant culture has denied the keys to many opportunities. Doors remain closed, so to speak, to the marginalized other. I will speak later of the ways that individuals in groups marginalized on the basis of difference can and do find solidarity in order to mitigate the harshness of the effects of being pushed to the periphery.[13]

Examining how stereotypic marginalization occurs in schools, Polakow provides poignant descriptions of schools where children are comprehended as entities with labels; the label becoming the defining characteristic of the child.[14] She records teacher conversations where children are classified, lumped together, and dismissed by use of labels such as "free lunchers," "those trailer park kids," "LD (learning disabled) and EI (emotionally impaired)," "project kids," or simply "these people." All these categories, either official or anecdotal, reduce children to a bundle of stereotypic characteristics. In the schools Polakow describes, the labels serve to dismiss any real learning potential. Instead, education (or miseducation) proceeds

> with the unquestioned assumption that the child must "fit" the classroom rather than the classroom should be made to "fit" the child, makes for a rigid, formalized curriculum and turns the developmental kindergarten into a training ground for compliance ... a receiving room for poor children whose economic disadvantage marks them as cognitively and socially deficient.[15]

Recall that the children of whom Polakow speaks in her research are five to ten years old. Marginalized by this labeling, they have little opportunity to gain the internal and external rewards from the endeavor of education. Unfortunately, we often have allowed ourselves to so marginalize persons based on such categories that we often never interact with persons in a personal and moral way, but simply respond to their category of difference and miss the meaning they give to their lives and to their particular differences. The categories themselves have become reified, as if they are somehow "out there," not to be instantiated in the distinctive ways particular persons might ascribe meaning to the characteristic.[16]

Consider this example of school use. In an introductory social studies textbook used in a large urban school district, the author divides the world into First, Second, Third, and now Fourth World countries. Note the language that he uses in describing the Fourth World:

> The Fourth World is made up of *hopeless have-not* countries. Bangladesh in Asia is an example of a Fourth World nation. The people of the Fourth World are the *most unfortunate of all*. They do *not have any hope* of achieving full development, because they are almost totally without resources.[17] (Emphasis mine)

Along with Bangladesh, the author includes many other countries such as Haiti, India, Egypt, and Lesotho, among others, as examples of Fourth World countries. Yet these are countries where people have rich histories and cultures and are working very hard to improve their nations. What kind of marginalizing is occurring here? First, individuals are made invisible as they are subsumed under someone's descriptive category. Second, the descriptive category sends pejorative messages as it describes a demographic and political category with personal terms such as *hopeless* and *have-nots*. Marginalization occurs as the individuals who live within the political borders of these nations are lumped together, categorized, and dismissed. Rather than calling these nations or their peoples "hopeless have-nots," I can imagine a rich discussion related to historical and political dominations, geopolitical resources, and culture that would describe the trying circumstances under which these countries struggle. Doing so would avoid categorical marginalization of the many peoples who live therein and would not pass on such damaging stereotypes to another generation of school children.

Responding to the challenge of living together in a diverse society and dealing with such reified stereotypes, Kwame Anthony Appiah cautions that we may simply be trading one tyranny with another when we let our individual identities be defined by how our larger group identity is characterized. Although Appiah is referring to the process of self-ascription of identity, he is cautioning against simply adopting those descriptions of one's identity defined by the culture at large. He states:

> Demanding respect for people as blacks and as gays requires that there are some scripts that go with being an African-American or having same-sex desires. There will be proper ways of being black and gay, there will be expectations to be met, demands will be made. It is at this point that someone who takes autonomy seriously will ask whether we have not replaced one kind of tyranny with another.[18]

To overcome marginalization at this level, we must of course see the differences, but we need to understand that it is the *individual* within a cultural context that gives particular meaning to what that difference means in his/her life. To do otherwise would be to employ a type of tyranny that marginalizes. To do otherwise would be to make that person invisible. As Collins indicates, treating an individual based upon stereotypical images created by the dominant culture makes that person "invisible as a fully human individual."[19] This is the devastation of marginalization.

To illustrate how categories of difference as imposed by others should not be construed as the sole definers of identity, I turn to an example employing the category of gender. The characteristic of gender can become a mechanism for the marginalization of girls and women when society employs it in the face of power differences. When gender is homogenous, such as in a group of women, then the character of gender marginalization changes. While the impact of gender marginalization cannot be thrown off at will, the significance of the ascribed difference is lessened. Yet if I am one of two women sitting in an advanced philosophy seminar among twelve men, my gender becomes distinctive and I, at least partially, define myself by that difference. Conversely, when I am in an advanced education seminar comprised mainly of women, the significance of my gender is lessened, though not invisible. In order to remedy and overcome a marginalization based on gender, I do not want the individual who marginalizes me to overlook that I am a woman (thereby bringing pieces of my culture's inheritance to that definition), but I want the individual who marginalizes me to realize that my gender category is not the only thing I am, that she/he should not respond to me only on the basis of this difference, and that fundamentally, I am the one who has the principal authority to determine the meaning I give to the category of my gender difference. It is this ability to define oneself to which Appiah was referring earlier. Dignity can be sustained only when these categories of difference are seen as protean concepts and when the primary meaning of one's life is understood as authored by oneself and respected by others.

While dichotomous subject-object thinking of the sort that Collins described based on categories of externally observable difference creates stereotypic marginalization, it also contributes to the type of marginalization that occurs at the psycho-social level. It is difficult to ascertain which form of marginalization is prior to the other. Both types of marginalization create circumstances where persons are "forced to exist only as a reflection in the eyes of others."[20] It is not fruitful to argue over which is worse; rather these marginalizations are best understood as interactive in nature. In other words, an individual who is stereotypically marginalized also can be psycho-socially marginalized, and when this occurs, various forms of domination and oppression are manifest. Not only does interaction imply a double challenge, but the interaction also can change the nature of the marginalization itself. We turn now to an examination of psycho-social marginalization.

PSYCHO-SOCIAL MARGINALIZATION

Psycho-social marginalization results when we are in relationships with others that require us to respond to them in a more personal way, yet we (consciously or not) marginalize them by not paying attention to the meaning that they are attempting to make. It is a type of marginalization that impacts personal identity development and meaning making. It is psychological in one sense because it impacts the deeply personal task of creating identity. It is also fundamentally social in that meaning must be created from within a social or relational realm, hence its name: psycho-social. In settings where individuals are expected to have some degree of intimacy that requires paying attention to the other, psycho-social marginalization occurs when attention is not given to the identity or meaning processes with which another may be engaged.

In the educational setting, psycho-social marginalization is more pervasive than stereotypic marginalization. It can affect those children who are stereotypically marginalized, as well as those who are not. It occurs when the meanings children ascribe in their lives are overlooked or dominated. As noted earlier, adults in schools have a distinctive moral obligation to the children there. School is a place where we have the opportunity to respond to others in this personal way. It is a realm that is half-way between private and public. It does not carry the obligation for full intimacy and responsibility that the family does, yet it is a place where more than the instrumental needs of the workplace bear sway. Schooling is a place where adults should be concerned with the flourishing of children's lives.

Because none of us enters education with a desire to marginalize children, it is important to consider ways that psycho-social marginalization occurs and impacts children in our schools. We need to look carefully at the ordinariness of our daily educational practice and ask ourselves if the schooling environment we create might not marginalize. It is not enough to identify "bad" teachers or administrators. This pervasive sense of marginalization can occur amidst the best intended teachers. I would like to point out areas where marginalization may occur in our practice. While they may seem similar, they have important, but subtle distinctions. I have identified five ways that psycho-social marginalization may occur in schools when the adults responsible for the education of children (1) fail to listen to the meaning a child attempts to convey, (2) ignore the already existent meaning of the child, (3) interrupt the holistic development of a child's life, (4) impose meaning without thoughtful deliberation, and (5) do not provide space for expression of the child's meaning. I will discuss each of these in turn with ordinary examples taken from the daily school life of our children.

First, marginalization occurs when we fail to listen to the meaning a child attempts to convey. There are many instances throughout the school day when children attempt to gain the attention of their teacher, for a variety of reasons and in a variety of ways. While a teacher cannot respond to every tap-tap on her shoulder, she must be concerned to listen for what each child is seeking. But this type of careful attention happens too few times in schools. For example, Maria approaches Mrs. Johnson's desk during math time and says she does not understand the assignment. Much to the surprise of Maria, Mrs. Johnson reprimands her first, for being out of her desk (she was supposed to raise her hand), and second, she tells Maria that if she had listened to the explanation given earlier, she would understand how to do the problem. Maria is then sent back to her seat, dismissed emotionally as well as intellectually. Why would a teacher act in this way? Perhaps it was a bad day, but in this particular class, it happened more than once. Most likely, this practice represented the teacher's attempt at classroom management, which is no easy task. But what we need to inquire about is what is lost in her attempt to manage the classroom in this manner. The meaning the individual student brings to her education is lost, and the teacher loses the ability to connect with the existing meaning-making framework of the child. In cases such as these, it is not just the individual student who is impacted, but because all actions take place on the stage of the classroom and are open for every student to see, the class receives a clear message. Such a management practice sends an unmistakable signal to all the students there. It is not safe to say, "I don't understand. Will you help me?"

In a similar example, students find themselves in a high school study hall where they have a reasonable rule that they must not be out of their seats wandering in the room. Yet if they have a legitimate need to speak with the teacher, they are reprimanded for raising their hands to ask him a question. Several students try to get their needs met (for going to the counselor or to take a make-up test in another classroom), but when met with a punitive response, the entire study hall quickly learns what is safe and what is not. The kids have a choice. They either grumble under their breath and gradually disengage from a school with such unfair and unexamined practices, or they rebel and cause all sorts of grief for the study hall teacher who in turn has his negative expectations of student behavior met. And so it goes. Within such a dichotomous framework (teacher v. student) alternative responses are not considered which creates a loss for the total community.

Second, marginalization occurs as one ignores the already existent meaning of the child or in other words, ignores how this experience is for the one who experiences it. This usually occurs when a teacher does not consider what a child already knows and thinks about a subject. Not all teachers plan their teaching content based upon the already existent knowledge, experience, and understandings of the class members. Some teachers do not inquire into what individual children know about a subject content area that they will be teaching in order to alter how they present their unit. The evaluation of student abilities each year in the fall focuses on the levels of reading, writing, and computing. Rarely does a teacher determine the subject content knowledge that the students have prior to outlining the curriculum. Have the kids already been presented three years of northwest native American curriculum? The salmon cycle? Or who in the class has important understandings to share about a particular unit of study? Instead, meanings that the children bring with them that are already in existence are often overlooked. Rather, what is considered is the material last year's teacher covered, not what understandings and knowledge the students have. This practice leads us to assume, for example, that second-grade children already covered a unit on families, so that third-grade children need to learn about communities. Then we proceed to give it to them, regardless of what they already know. And usually those who know something get the high marks (for already knowing it!), and those who know little and have a long way to go get the low marks!

Third, psycho-social marginalization occurs when we interrupt the holistic development of a life by imposing a strong public/private split. This occurs most often when the world of home is separated from the world of school, thereby not acknowledging strong feelings that come with life experiences usually occurring in the private realm. These include deaths, births, weddings, divorces, as well as the more mundane things of life. They include the child's social world outside of school, or even the limited world of the classroom. By forcing a strong split between school and the children's other worlds, one interrupts the ability for educational meaning to become contextualized. Such a split often thwarts learning. For example, Lucy McCormick Calkins tells about what happened to one fourth-grade teacher when she began to use stories of life experiences that reflected the sadness often experienced in children's lives. "I think I'd been pretending that stories have happy endings, and reading those sad books, it tapped into the pain in the children's lives and in mine."[21] Up to this point, this particular teacher felt that getting her kids to write fluently in Writer's Workshop was like pulling teeth. It seemed stilted and artificial. But then she began reading a children's novel that had a sad ending, something she had shied away from in the past because she was worried that it might stir up difficult emotions or reveal private details of lives. She overlooked that the children were already living such lives full of emotion and personal feelings! She was amazed by the reactions of the children and the subsequent impact it had on their writing. What was once difficult and wearing now became fluid and fresh. She said:

> Stories and images cascaded over each other that morning. There was, in that room, a tumbling richness of stories, one resonating

against another, some dichotomous, some overlapping, but always gathering abundantly, and there was laughter too, and people listening to each other with tears brimming. There were exclamations of "That happened to me, too," and "You must have some family." There was among us a growing sense of "Here we stand, in the presence of life itself," of "What a privilege it is to be part of this community," of "What voices, what stories, what lives."[22]

She reported that the classroom came alive. It "bristle[d] with meaning." It was the way their teacher used stories that gave the children permission to bridge that huge gap between what happens to them "out there," out of school, and what goes on in the hours they sit in the classroom.

Fourth, imposing meaning without thoughtful deliberation can engender psycho-social marginalization. Notice that imposing meaning is not prohibited, but one must ask, upon what grounds and under what conditions may I impose? For after all, education implies a sharing or giving. Again, in Dewey's account, it implies a gain or growth or capacity for a future gain based on past experience. But given that a teacher has an understanding of what the classroom should be like, he or she must take careful steps to avoid the type of imposition that dominates a child's own meaning. The meaning a teacher brings should help a child's meaning expand and consider possibilities for how his or her world could be. That is what we would wish for, but generally what happens is that a meaning external to the child is imposed without forethought. Often this type of marginalization occurs in our nation's elite private schools. Students are socialized to accept a narrow meaning of achievement and success that a particular parent and school community have defined, often at the cost of any meaning that the child could possibly bring. Hence, students sometimes will prepare for careers in fields that might provide economic success, but have little personal meaning in their lives. At times and for some students, denying a part of themselves that is perhaps artistic or creative in return for business or engineering career goals puts a great deal of stress on them and manifests in emotional illness, alcohol, and drug abuse and tragically enough, suicide. In their study of elite prep schools, Cookson and Persell remark that "the stripping away of the private self that is essential for the prep rite of passage is but the first step in a lifetime of personal denial and the denial of the person."[23] It is this separation of the person/personal from the process of education that warrants the claim that marginalization and hence miseducation is taking place.

As teachers, our educational traditions impose meanings that we may not even realize. For example, when we create and exhibit a comparison chart posting stars by students' names as they learn their multiplication tables, we are putting a meaning on what is deemed to be academic success. More than that, we are assenting to academic competitiveness wherein there are winners and losers. While all eventually may learn their multiplication tables through the twelves, in every chart there are those who soar ahead and those who fall farther behind. Grades, the topics of study we choose, those we leave out, the insult one child may give to another that goes unchallenged by us—all these practices provide our students with clear, implicit messages about the meaning that we as teachers and as schools value. This is not to say that grades or multiplication star charts cannot be used appropriately. Rather, it is my intent to ask each of us as educators to examine our practices very carefully and measure them against whether or not they assist children's dignity to flourish.

Fifth, marginalization may occur when we fail to provide space for the expression of a child's meaning. If every part of the school day is used up by a prescribed curriculum and if every unit for the year is preplanned, then where is the space for the expression of the child's meaning? This notion of having "space for expression" connotes the amount of time a teacher may employ, but it also speaks to the physical configuration of the classroom and school and how the learning process itself is undertaken. Just recently, I was surprised to see that a middle school social studies teacher purposely left an entire unit open for the students to determine their own course of study. This came toward the end of the year, after they had developed as a class community and had respect for their shared learning environment. What a vote of confidence this teacher gave these young people! The message she gave was one of confidence in the students' ability to define and share the journey of exploring their world.

What often passes for education is the rote memorization of things already known, maps already made, diagrams already drawn. Essayist Andrei Codrescu, makes the following observation that illustrates the waste of always approaching the curriculum in the same way:

> Millions of frogs, snakes, and turtles are ripped open every year in classrooms so that kids can see what's inside. We already know

what's inside, so what's the point in looking and looking and killing and killing? Kids can see pictures of what's inside. At LSU where I work we have a cow with a window in her stomach. You can look in the window while the cow walks around and you can see the guts all coiled up and huge wads of grass being turned into beer or something. Why can't the same be done with one frog or one snake or one turtle instead of having to waste millions of them?[24]

This is not to say that knowing about the insides of frogs is not important, but it is to question the convention of always doing it in the same, redundant way. From this passage, we get the impression that Codrescu cares about what happens to the frogs. But we can just as well ask what happens to the children when there are no open spaces to learn about frogs in some other way. A teacher concerned with providing space for the expression of children's meaning might by-pass cutting up frogs (look at a poster of what is inside) and then proceed by asking, What are other ways of knowing about frogs? Imagine the learning places that might open! By creating spaces where students do not simply engage in rote memorization or tasks, students are more apt to have the opportunity to imbue their own learning with meaning.

In summary, psycho-social marginalization is fundamentally devastating because it impacts the very development of the self in a way that stereotypic marginalization does not. It can result when educators engage in the following: (1) do not listen to the meaning a child is attempting to convey; (2) ignore the already existent meaning of the child; (3) interrupt the holistic development of a child's life; (4) impose meaning without thoughtful deliberation, and (5) not provide space for expression of the child's meaning. All of these descriptions of psycho-social marginalization close avenues for meaning and hence the ever-unfolding story of a life to grow and develop in children's experience.

MARGINALIZATION AND THE NEED FOR NARRATIVE RESOURCES

In order to curtail the impacts of marginalization, it is important to recognize that the depth and breadth of narrative language and experience in schools are necessary for selves to develop and flourish. This is so because the marginalization described herein is embedded within a narrative form. It requires language of some sort. The stories of our lives require narrative expressions. If the self is created in large part through comprehending experience as narrative (as I shall argue in chapter 4), then it follows that when identity development and meaning-making experiences are curtailed, the identity and development of the self also are curtailed and sparse. Marginalization occurs, and dignity is diminished. When the environment marginalizes by not providing for rich narrative experiences, then the meaning and identity that developing selves are making withers. These fundamental tasks of development are ignored, and the individual child is marginalized as he or she is held in abeyance of the task of identity development and meaning making as the central tasks of the self. We have done what Collins indicated occurs with external indicators such as race, class, and gender: we have dichotomized the situation. But in this case of psycho-social marginalization, we erroneously have separated the child as meaning maker from the "child as learner." In so doing, we have construed the "child as learner" simply as a vessel to be filled with facts. This kind of pedagogy can be described best as a traditional form of education, where as Freire describes it, we "turn (students) into 'containers,' into 'receptacles,' to be 'filled' by the teacher. The more completely he fills the receptacles, the better teacher he is. The more meekly the receptacles permit themselves to be filled, the better students they are."[25]

In contrast to the type of education that sees the child as an empty vessel to be filled with knowledge, and in order to minimize psycho-social marginalization, we must employ a notion of education that acknowledges that the dignity of the self can flourish only as individuals are free to draw upon a rich cultural language wherein identity and meaning can flourish. Therefore, if we are concerned with the dignity of children or their ability to author their own lives, we will ensure that individuals have available to them and are free to draw upon a rich language in the development of their lives and have this narrative meaning understood as an integral part of who they are and what they are to be about when they walk through the school doors. To do otherwise is to marginalize persons psycho-socially in a fundamental way because to do otherwise interrupts the development of a life story.

We cannot ignore the fact that the realm of schooling serves children in their development. We cannot send them to school for six or more hours a day immersed as they are in the mesh of human relationships and say that the only function for schools is to teach the "3 R's," while we reserve the hours away from school (hours where children are typically tutored by commercial television) for paying attention to human development. In addition, it is unreasonable to expect that children can turn off their development and identity-making processes for the hours they sit in school. Imagine the silliness of such a request!

Unfortunately, we have a fairly good example of what that may look like when we recall the traditional junior high structure. In that context, it appears that we have asked children to divorce themselves from the demands of their identity making as they make the transition from elementary to early adolescent education. The structure of the traditional junior high seems antithetical to the developmental needs of the child. In effect, we are asking students to divorce their developmental needs from their academic and school needs. Forcing this split between developmental needs and institutional structure is a form of marginalization because we are pushing to the periphery or margin their central developmental tasks. Does such a set-up work very well? Ask most educators about teaching kids from ages twelve through fourteen! Junior high school teachers are either revered by their colleagues for their bravery, or eyes are rolled as the teacher says, "I could never teach that age!" The difficulty of the developmental tasks of adolescence is being compounded by the educational structure that does not fit the developmental needs. Thankfully, some of these structural concerns are being addressed in the middle-school configuration.[26]

To end the psycho-social marginalization that occurs in schools, we need to view the first priority of education as one that nurtures narrative identity making. At their foundation, schools would be a noninstrumental realm where identity development and meaning making needs determine the character of the rest of the educational program. From a position based on a commitment to identity development and meaning making, schools could then identify and build what may be considered the instrumental tasks of education. But to date, neglecting a focus on dignity, schools have marginalized students. This psycho-social marginalization is more devastating than stereotypic for two reasons. First, with psycho-social marginalization, there are no opportunities to create a solidarity that could mitigate against the invisibility of not acknowledging the meaning a student creates. With psycho-social marginalization, invisibility is compounded by isolation. Second, stereotypic marginalization pushes one to the periphery of a given activity, and what is lost is the opportunity to gain the benefits of a given activity. But with psycho-social marginalization, one is pushed to the periphery of those activities where one has the opportunity to develop one's self. Stereotypic marginalization puts the goods of society at risk, whereas psycho-social puts the development of the self at risk.[27] As discussed earlier, education must contain a concern with development of the self, for example, the capacity and opportunity to create one's life. Hence, students are marginalized in schools when schools operate in a manner external to the students' understandings and development. If schools function externally to students' understandings and development, they are not educating the students. Therefore, if students are marginalized, then they are not educated. Rather, miseducation is taking place.

RESISTING MARGINALIZATION

What are possible responses to marginalization? When persons are marginalized, either stereotypically or psycho-socially, they can internalize the message of the marginalizer, attempt to ignore it, or they can resist the attempt to push them to the margins. When resistance occurs as a response to marginalization, it is a claim for autonomy, for example, for the ability to either define the terms of one's own difference (as Appiah described earlier) or to have recognition for the meaning one is creating. Too often those who dominate misjudge the resistance response. If the resistance response incorporates some form of collective solidarity, this often is judged as hostility, aggressiveness, or unwillingness to compromise. If the resistance is individual in nature, it is often judged to be a psychological problem or as a deficiency in character. For example, in *I Won't Learn from You*, Herbert Kohl tells of the grandfather of one of his fifth-grade students. Wilfredo, the grandfather, refused to learn to speak English and insisted upon communicating only in Spanish.[28] While others attributed Wilfredo's refusal to a "cover-up of either his fear of trying to learn English or his failure to do so," Kohl came to understand that the grandfather was concerned that his family and their attendant language, customs, and culture would be lost if they did not carefully sustain their own language. Not only did the attributions of fear or failure miss the point, as Kohl tells us, but they also "show a lack of respect for Wilfredo's ability to judge what is appropriate learning for himself and for his grandchildren." Wilfredo is claiming the autonomy necessary to resist the marginalization of him as carrier of his culture. Not only did this marginalization miss the point of Wilfredo's autonomy, but the attribution of failure "turned a cultural problem into a personal psychological problem: [it] turned willed refusal to learn into failure to learn." When this resistance is understood as a personal psychological problem, it is only a small step to dismissing the individual as pathological. Again, the individual's meaning and any legitimate concern that is raised are made invisible.

If an individual does not resist marginalization, but instead internalizes the message of the dominator, Kohl indicates that the "results of failure are most often a loss of self-confidence accompanied by a sense of inferiority and inadequacy." The individual has succumbed to pressures external to him or herself. Many times though, education simply proceeds along the lines of the status quo. Students go to school, and then they go home. There is nothing special occurring at school that ties students to it or to the adults there. Perhaps students are soaking up the message that the meaning they make in their lives is of little importance. Perhaps they have strong support systems in place that counteract the negative messages of marginalization. Lacking knowledge of this, we need to ask if we are willing to take the risk of being unsure about what students are doing with marginalizing messages.

To be sure, some students do resist marginalization, and in so doing place themselves outside of the educational system. Still, such resistance has its benefits. Kohl states that resistance "tends to strengthen the will, clarify one's definition of self, reinforce self-discipline, and provide inner satisfaction." That does not mean that there will not be societal costs to pay, but holding on to one's integrity in the face of marginalization has powerful consequences for one's identity. In fact, according to Kohl, it is a sane response to the crazy-making nature of marginalization. Descriptions of such resistance bring to mind the powerful images of Rosa Parks, Martin Luther King, Jr., and Nelson Mandela. Dr. King speaks eloquently about the moral call to maladjust to immoral actions.

Modern psychology has a word that is probably used more than any other word. It is the word "maladjusted." Now we all should seek to live a well-adjusted life in order to avoid neurotic and schizophrenic personalities. But there are some things within our social order to which I am proud to be maladjusted. I never intend to adjust myself to segregation and discrimination. I never intend to adjust myself to mob rule. I never intend to adjust myself to the tragic effects of the methods of physical violence and to tragic militarism. I call upon you to be maladjusted to such things.[29]

Viewed in this way, there are reasons why many students maladjust to schooling that may exclude them in the ways previously mentioned and exhibit that maladjustment as resistance to teachers' efforts.

Resistance either to psycho-social or to stereotypic marginalization produces different impacts. Understanding this is also a key to understanding why psycho-social marginalization is often more devastating than stereotypic. For example, in *Domination and the Arts of Resistance,* James Scott argues that marginalization along the categories of race, class, and gender (stereotypic marginalization) can be moderated through forms of group resistance. Scott explains the relationship between domination and subordination by utilizing a notion of transcript. Understanding that there are two transcripts, one public and one hidden, assists us in seeing how those authoring the hidden transcript resist marginalization by a dominant culture. Scott argues that the dominant group creates a public transcript that is to account for the way things are. He refers to the public transcript as the "self-portrait of dominant elites as they would have themselves seen, . . . designed to be impressive, to affirm and naturalize the power of the dominant elites, and to conceal or euphemize the dirty linen of their rule."[30] Likewise, the subordinate group creates a hidden transcript that gives voice to the frustration and feeling of powerlessness that living with domination brings. He indicates that the hidden transcript is the "privileged site for nonhegemonic, contrapuntl [sic], dissident, subversive discourse" and that creating spaces for these hidden transcripts to be created, expressed, and nourished is an avenue for those marginalized to resist the labels of the marginalizer.[31]

The space afforded by the hidden transcripts allows for room to play and try out meanings and identities. It also creates a space without marginalization where one's sense of identity can remain intact and continue to develop, thus preventing psycho-social marginalization. To illustrate how this can occur, I draw upon the experience of bell hooks. She describes the power of her rural, southern, black community. True to Scott's analysis, it is a place where a hidden transcript thrived. Although living in an overtly racist time, hooks indicated that the way of being in community allowed the space for identity and meaning to be defined by those who lived there, rather than by the hegemonic discourse. She describes the "experience of rural living, poverty, racial segregation, and resistance struggle." So although her rural community faced horrendous stereotypic marginalization, it was able to prevent psycho-social marginalization. Her world, a space for hidden transcripts, allowed the following resistance to occur:

> That way "downhome" black folks had of speaking to one another, looking one another directly in the eye (many of us had old folks tell us, don't look down, look at me when I'm talking to you) was not some quaint country gesture. It was a practice of resistance undoing years of racist teachings that had denied us the power of recognition, the power of gaze. These looks were affirmations of our being, a balm to wounded spirits. They opposed the internalized racism or alienated individualism that would have us turn away from one another, aping the dehumanizing practices of the colonizer.[32]

This space, free from the domination of the oppressor's categories, provided the individual room for self-definition.

In contrast to the impacts of stereotypic marginalization, resisting psycho-social marginalization presents problems. What makes it troubling is that there is no group or culture to which one may turn to find space away from the oppressor's gaze that allows for hidden transcripts and development of identity. When psycho-social marginalization occurs, except for a few cases, it isolates. Compare the account that Richard Wright gives of growing up in the South to that of bell hooks. While hooks had the larger community to mitigate the harshness of stereotypic marginalization, Wright had nowhere to turn to find a space where he could create his life and thus sustain his dignity. He writes:

> Not only had the southern whites not known me, but, more important still, as I had lived in the South I had not had the chance to learn who I was. The pressure of southern living kept me from being the kind of person that I might have been. I had been what my surroundings had demanded, what my family—conforming to the dictates of the whites above them—had exacted of me, and what the whites had said that I must be. Never being fully able to be myself, I had slowly learned that the South could recognize but a part of a man, could accept but a fragment of his personality, and all the rest—the best and deepest things of heart and mind— were tossed away in blind ignorance and hate.[33]

We can now apply this understanding of the isolating effects of psycho-social marginalization to what occurs in schools. Consider this example. Recall Kohl, who provides a description of the "not-learning" response of young people who are marginalized. First, he indicates that students who are refusing to learn as an "appropriate response to oppressive education" may exhibit the following behaviors:

> Many youngsters who ask impertinent questions, listen to their teachers in order to contradict them, and do not take homework or tests seriously are practiced not-learners. The quieter not-learners sit sullenly in class, daydreaming and shutting out the sound of their teacher's voice. They sometimes fall off their chairs or throw things across the room or resort to other strategies of disruption. Some push things so far that they get put in special classes or get thrown out of school.[34]

Students who find themselves psycho-socially marginalized from their own educations have little recourse or place to go where the meaning they are attempting to convey can be acknowledged. As adults entrusted with the moral responsibilities attendant in education, we are derelict if we automatically attribute the problem to the child. When we make that attribution, "resistance and rebellion is stigmatized. The system's problem becomes the victim's problem." The failure is attributed to the student, and the institution of schooling remains intact. The root causes of the marginalization go unchallenged.

The "not-learning" response that Kohl describes is simply another form of resistance to the marginalization and affront to the dignity of the young person.[35] When we allow these external indicators of behavior to substitute for causes of behavior, then education has been "reduced to a pressure from without" as Dewey cautioned us it would. When this occurs, a student can respond only to external directives. There is no room for his or her own internal understandings to direct the process of education. Being marginalized from the process of education itself, students have diminished resources for their on-going attempts to create identity and meaning. Hence, with few strategies for resistance, children who encounter psycho-social marginalization face a loss of self.

In summary, I have described three possible responses to either stereotypic or psycho-social marginalization. Individuals can internalize the message of the marginalizer, attempt to ignore it, or resist the attempt to push them to the margin. Noting the role of the hidden transcript allows me to make an important point. If an individual who experiences oppressive stereotypic marginalization has a cultural space where an active hidden transcript occurs, then this space allows for a challenge to any psycho-social marginalization. It does this by virtue of the ascriptions that others can give the child to counteract the message of psycho-social marginalization. Unfortunately for children who do not have a place where there is a hidden transcript to counteract other marginalizing experiences, psycho-social marginalization results without the mediation and protection of the hidden transcript. There is a possibility that children who are stereotypically marginalized will be able to counteract a message of psycho-social marginalization because they have a hidden transcript active in their lives. Without this, psycho-social marginalization remains horribly damaging as it affects the development of the self.

BREAKING THE FICTION

While Scott maintains that the ongoing arena of resistance surrounds the interaction between the public and hidden transcripts, he notes that there are electrifying times when the hidden transcript is spoken for the first time in public.[36] He indicates that the reversal of public humiliation and degradation must also be public in order to restore dignity that has been affronted in a public space.[37] The "breaking of the public fiction" allows for a psychological release by breaking the silence and subsequently allowing a recreation of social meaning. Solidarity or community can be borne from the knowledge of the shared hidden transcript, and when persons speak aloud what heretofore has been relegated to secretive spaces, they are bequeathed a sense of wholeness and dignity. In this way, persons so marginalized can resist the dignity-destructive impact of practices that dominate. In like manner, the effort to overcome marginalization of young people must incorporate a willingness to break those "public fictions" that perpetuate marginalization in schools.

While Scott's work speaks to the adult realm of current and historical domination and prejudice, we may glean some important understandings for our discussion of marginalization in the schools. Are there "hidden transcripts" in our schools today? One can answer this by looking for spaces where meanings of young people, the children in our schools, can be voiced. In *36 Children*, Herbert Kohl suggests that recess may be such a space where children can find and develop a place for their voices.[38] Certainly, there are other age-appropriate "hidden transcripts" that represent healthy developmental features of gaining independence from parents and other adults. In this regard, I think of games of note passing and adolescent conversations about the demands of school and how those conversations take on a decidedly different character when adults are present! But, when considering the serious problem of marginalization, perhaps one would want to discover whether children in schools have a voice in determining what their education should entail. Are there places where students who assuredly have opinions on the subject can challenge the necessity of keeping such conversations hidden? In other words, are there ways that children, parents, or teachers can break those fictions that marginalize students?

Certainly, there are "public fictions" (portions of the public transcript that maintain marginalization) that deserve to be broken in schools today. We need to challenge the public fiction apparent in the labels given students in the schools that Polakow describes. Not understanding that much of schooling marginalizes children's identity and meaning is another public fiction that deserves to be broken. Along with these two fictions is the notion that the problem belongs to the child more than to the institution. This, too, deserves to be broken. What is more important, Scott provides us an insight for how one can develop a solidarity or, in educational terms, build a learning community. In order to do this, the transcripts, both public and hidden, must be shared. First, there must be an understanding that "hidden transcripts" and their concomitant "public fictions" exist. Second, there must be spaces for dialogue that could challenge and subsequently recreate a public transcript that is less marginalizing.

Engagement in such a dialogue necessarily would create a new public transcript for education, it is hoped. one that is devoid of damaging fictions. If we are concerned with not marginalizing the children in our schools, we must spend some time exploring what a life not marginalized might look like. In what state do we want to find our children (and ourselves), if it is not one of marginalization? It is to this question that we now turn.

4

THE ROLE OF DIGNITY:
Nurturing the Narrative Self

DIGNITY AND THE SELF

As I argued in chapter 1, the moral dimension of education requires that the dignity of children be sustained. In order to support this claim, I must first provide an account of what I mean by dignity and why it is important that it is sustained in the lives of children at school. As Vivian Paley has described, "What happens . . . in schools is the mirror of its moral landscape."[1] This landscape is expansive in that it encompasses the multiple dimensions of schools, from the content of what is taught to the quality and quantity of relationships between adults and children and between students themselves; the structure of the day; the look of the hallways; and the greetings from the staff, including custodians, secretaries, and lunch workers. It is the "experience" of schooling in its sum total. This experience can be either the site for the flourishing or the degradation of a child's dignity.

Dignity may be understood as either the inherent value and worth of each human life or as an ethical construct wherein we ascribe value to ourselves and others. Either way, moral responsibilities attend. The latter concept of dignity consists of two aspects. I call the first aspect "personal dignity" in that it represents the dignity of each individual. I refer to the second aspect of dignity as "relational dignity." Relational dignity carries with it a moral obligation to acknowledge the personal dignity of each individual. It is relational, because dignity is only fully sustained through a particular type of participation in our social or relational realm. Dignity is deeply social in its sources. It is bestowed and diminished in the context of social relationships. Therefore, the experience of dignity is both an individual and a social concern because the acknowledgment of personal dignity necessarily occurs within a web of social relationships. Let me explain further.

Although dignity is impossible to attain outside of its relational sense, it is possible to have personal dignity when the social acknowledgment inherent in relational dignity is severely diminished. Though difficult, one can sustain personal dignity in the face of overriding threats to dignity through self-ascriptions that may have developed from early relationships and/or the hidden transcripts of one's culture. When confronted with messages that attempt to marginalize, one can respond to these negative messages by telling oneself something along the lines of, "I am a person of value and deserve the rights accorded to any human being." For example, during the civil rights movement, Rosa Parks defied the law by not moving to the back of the bus. She provided a public demonstration of how one can sustain her own dignity in the face of marginalization. Confronted with the overwhelming social message that she was not valued the same as whites, Rosa Parks sustained her own dignity enough to overcome these negative messages and remain seated at the front of the bus. Among other things, she relied on a hidden transcript and a deep sense of personal dignity that most likely originated within her familial and cultural context.

We can imagine a second scenario. A child is labeled "Chapter 1" in school and pulled out for compensatory education every day. Imagine that the attitudes of teachers and peers surrounding this intervention were not good, but were negative and stereotypical, as they sometimes can be. If a child had a strong enough sense of self, he or she might not be battered down by the label, the experience, and the social expectations. Instances such as these two are the exception. And, in fact, in each case, the individual most likely persisted because somewhere in his or her life the individual had or were receiving messages that sustained and nurtured his or her personal dignity. In special cases it is possible to sustain one's own personal dignity in the face of overwhelming messages to the contrary.

Too many times children are damaged by the marginalizing messages they receive at school, many of which are subtle and pervasive in the institutional setting itself. It is not easy to counteract negative messages continually; and, of course, the challenge is amplified for children who are in the process of developing their identities. Self-ascriptions of dignity are unlikely if the adults involved in children's lives do not help them learn why and how to make such ascriptions. As I will discuss later in this chapter, this is so because the self is dialogical in nature and narrative in expression, and the identity and meaning that the self creates are dependent upon the social relationships which one experiences. Hence, the focus in this work will be on what I am calling the "relational sense" of dignity.

It seems reasonable to say that dignity respects the value of each human life. But what else can we say about that? What would this respect entail? As I have already argued in chapter 2, dignity represents a responsibility to recognize one's right to create one's own original life. This is the relationship between dignity and the self. Daniel Pekarsky sheds light on what it might mean to respect the tasks of being human:

> To regard a person as a human being is to be mindful of the fact that he is a creature struggling to weave together a meaningful life that grows out of his understandings and speaks to his interests and concerns; and it is to be concerned lest we arbitrarily interfere with his efforts to shape the direction of his life or adversely affect the way he feels about himself and his situation. The intuitive notion here is that to regard a person as a human being is to address him with a measure of respect.[2]

Given that the creation of a life involves the creation of meaning and identity, dignity must respect these focal tasks of the self. Without developing meaning and identity, there would be no selves and the question of sustaining dignity would become moot.

Nurturing dignity would entail providing the room for selves to create their lives. In some instances, as Pekarsky implies, this would entail *not* interfering with people's lives so that they are free to pursue what avenues they will. But in other cases, dignity would entail being involved in the process. Education certainly represents one of these cases of being involved in creating a life.

I propose that education represents a case for the nurturance of dignity because engaging in the process of education already demonstrates a proactive stance regarding what we think children should know and why it would be good for them to know it. This proactive stance condones involvement in the process of education and the institution of schooling generally. Because of the moral obligation between adult and child, and because schooling already purports to "interfere" in the lives of children in order to educate them, attention must be paid to the quality of the interactions that occur there. If we were concerned with not interfering with others' lives in order to provide them the greatest possible "freedom" to develop their lives, then we would not even condone education. Certainly education is an interference, albeit a positive one, in the lives of children. How that education occurs, its purposes and aims, is a matter for social and ethical inquiry and dialogue. In order that we might be prepared to address the character of what education should be, we need to provide a rich account of what dignity means.

Important to any discussion about dignity and children's lives, recall that sustaining dignity means more than simply preserving it when it is found. Sustaining the dignity of the child would include the active creation of environments where meaning and identity could develop. It would ask adults to teach children how to make ascriptions of dignity to themselves and others. The concept of dignity is not static, but is one that requires building, growing, and protecting a sense of dignity for the self. Understanding this also allows me to talk of *nurturing* dignity. In the lives of children, this seems appropriate. Most of us share some form of a common commitment to the care of children. Individually and as a society, we recoil at accounts of child abuse, homelessness, drug abuse, and poverty that harm children. We accept some notion of a mutual obligation to protect and nurture their lives. In being concerned with the well-being of children's lives, we are concerned with their dignity.

Having the autonomy to create and develop one's life implies freedom. While dignity connotes a sense of freedom, I contend that not just any interpretation of freedom is implied in dignity. There are three qualities that characterize the type of freedom that gives breadth to our understanding of dignity. They are (1) that freedom implies authentic authorship; (2) that the achievement of freedom is always relational in nature; and (3) that it is always instantiated in particular lives, rather than as an abstract ideal. These qualities prevent the notion of freedom from being defined solely as noninterference in one's choices and life plans. It also negates a belief in educational neutrality. No matter how hard we may try to cast education as a neutral endeavor that teaches skills only (reading, writing, and arithmetic), it simply is always much more than this. For example, consider Ira Shor's point:

> A curriculum that avoids questioning school and society is not, as is commonly supposed, politically neutral. It cuts off the students' development as critical thinkers about their world. If the students' task is to memorize rules and existing knowledge, without questioning the subject matter or the learning process, their potential for critical thought and action will be restricted. . . . A curriculum that does not challenge the standard syllabus and conditions in society informs students that knowledge and the world are fixed and are fine the way they are, with no role for students to play in transforming them, and no need for change.[3]

Given that schools can never operate from a neutral stance, the question becomes from what position should they operate? Being part of a society with a commitment to democracy provides some guidelines for us, but we must openly dialogue about what values are nurtured by our educational practice. A commitment to the flourishing of lives through attending to their dignity is congruent with democracy and may be its underlying tenet. This distinction is crucial in order to support my account of dignity.

The first characteristic of freedom implied in relational dignity includes honoring the autonomy of oneself and others, whereby one is deemed the author of one's own life. Being the author of one's own life implies a sense of authenticity, because it ascribes voice to the one whose life it is. Authenticity enjoins one to speak to how life is experienced by oneself. In *The Ethics of Authenticity*, Charles Taylor defines authenticity as the following: "There is a certain way of being human that is *my* way. I am called upon to live my life in this way, and not in imitation of anyone else's. But this gives a new importance to being true to myself. If I am not, I miss the point of my life, I miss what being human is for *me*."[4]

So authorship and authenticity complement each other. An authentic authorship strives to give expression to what life means for oneself. Authorship and authenticity speak to the tasks of self-development, that is, identity development and meaning making. But in order not to fall into narcissistic explanations of self-development, Taylor further states that this project of discovering what life is for oneself must not be undertaken in an isolated manner. "I can define my identity only against the background of things that matter," argues Taylor.[5] To say that one is the author of one's own life does not disregard the relational nature of the self. This is so because "things that matter" include the lives of others, history, tradition, culture, and more. One is not alone in creating a life. In order to be engaged in such a process, education should provide students with many opportunities to cross paths with the things that matter. Education should be rich with the stories and cultural traditions of ourselves and diverse others.

The second characteristic of freedom implied by dignity also draws on its relational nature. Relational dignity would challenge the notion of freedom as lack of interference and a mindset that advocates, "Every man for himself!" To the contrary, in *Rethinking Democracy*, Carol Gould indicates that freedom must be understood as more than just unfettered choice; it should be experienced "as an activity of self-development." She remarks as well that freedom is necessarily social in nature; it "entails that social cooperation is a necessary condition for self-development."[6] Her notion of freedom as self-development that requires social cooperation buttresses my account of dignity as social and relational in nature with attendant obligations to one another. This second sense of freedom fits well for our involvement in education. After all, while deeply personal, education almost always takes place relationally. At a minimum, we know that schooling provides a social setting that could support education, which nurtures dignity. Too often, though, schools are sites for competitive and individualistic achievement, rather than experiences where learning is relational in nature. For example, from elementary school through the university, students do exercises in classrooms that are turned in to teachers for their eyes only. Why not share the results of student learning with one another through presentations, invitations to other classes, demonstrations, book making, videos, and other forms of expression that are relational in nature? Children are curious about one another, and this curiosity can be another asset in the search for educative experiences.

Adding to this rich understanding of freedom is the third characteristic of particularity. In *The Dialectic of Freedom*, Maxine Greene argues that freedom means paying attention to the particular. It is not just an abstraction. She states:

A free act, after all, is a particularized one. It is undertaken from the standpoint of a particular, situated person trying to bring into existence something contingent on his/her hopes, expectations, and capacities. The world in which the person creates and works through a future project cannot but be a social world; and the nature of the project cannot but be affected by shared meanings and interpretations of existing social realities.[7]

This enriched understanding of freedom that Greene describes gives depth to the notion of dignity. In Gould's notion of relation, we see that dignity in its fullest sense cannot simply mean being left alone to do as one wills. If freedom is an aspect of dignity, and as freedom requires a deeply social and contextualized experience, then dignity as well must be realized in a deeply social and contextualized fashion. Therefore, sustaining dignity by paying attention to *particularized* individuals necessitates paying attention to their particular story as an account of what life means for them. Sustaining dignity relies on an understanding of freedom that grants authorship to individuals to be free to be the meaning makers of their own lives. It recognizes that freedom is realized only within particular lives and contexts.

Schools are institutions and, as such, often have their own policies. While policies can offer some forms of institutional fairness, they also can interfere with the needed attention to particular lives. One reason why we find we need such rules and policies is because many times our schools serve five hundred, a thousand, two thousand, or more students. How could we pay attention to the particular? This is one of the premiere reasons why Deborah Meier, in describing the success of Central Park East schools says that the one aspect of their school about which they would not compromise is size.[8] Size allows many things to occur that would become very difficult otherwise. We need not let the structure of our buildings prevent us from getting to the particular because, as many are doing, we may simply create schools within schools!

Before moving on, I should draw a connection here between dignity and marginalization. Because psycho-social marginalization is destructive of personal identity and meaning, it is an affront to dignity since dignity requires that the creation of one's life be honored. When marginalization interrupts that process, dignity cannot be achieved because the creation of a life encompasses those processes of personal identity and meaning making. Therefore, marginalization is the antithesis of dignity. Understanding how dignity can be sustained requires acknowledging the dialogical and narrative nature of human experience. I turn now to this discussion.

DIGNITY AND THE DIALOGICAL NATURE OF THE SELF

Understanding how dignity can be nurtured in the lives of children requires an understanding of the self that encompasses both the personal and the social. In other words, in attending to dignity, we acknowledge the dialogical interplay of human relations as a condition for creating a life. It can be done in no other way. Kwame Anthony Appiah describes the dual nature of the self as follows. "Each person's individual identity is seen as having two major dimensions. There is a collective dimension, the intersection of their collective identities, and there is a personal dimension, consisting of other socially or morally important features—intelligence, charm, wit, cupidity—that are not themselves the basis of forms of collective identity."[9] While collective identity making is also an important part of the personal dimension of identity making, it is the domain in which stereotypical marginalization occurs since it ostensibly involves a grouping or categorizing of persons on the basis of a generalized, single characteristic. The collective or relational sphere is also the place for the converse to occur, that is, the bestowing of dignity throughout daily moral interactions. Hence, paying attention to dignity requires that we create a context for the dialogical development of the self to occur; or, in other words, it requires that we create an environment where marginalization on either the social or the personal plane does *not* occur. Knowing that part of who we are is created through a collective identity-making process helps us discern how sustaining dignity encompasses both the personal and the social. Dignity is ascribed to others in our midst as we honor and respect the ever-ongoing activity of creating a life.

Throughout this discussion I will refer to the self as an individual, although I also recognize that the degree to which the individual is considered autonomous or relational is culturally constructed.[10] While preserving the notion of a discrete self as author of a life, I utilize a more relational notion of the self than traditional liberalism most likely would claim. The discrete self I describe is discrete only insofar as the emotion, the body, cognition, and psychological structures that define it *feel* that it is a unique self. Beyond this, I accept that we never create ourselves in isolation.

Rather, we require and dignity demands rich, dialogical experiences. Drawing upon the ideas of Bakhtin, Charles Taylor describes the "dialogical self" that is created only in interaction with others within a cultural context. Saying that we are dialogically created means that the self is immersed within the web of the human condition. Taylor ascribes to human life a "fundamentally dialogical character." What this means and how it relates to the importance of the self is seen in the following excerpt:

> We become full human agents, capable of understanding ourselves, and hence of defining an identity, through our acquisition of rich human languages of expression. . . . But we are inducted into these in exchange with others. No one acquires the languages needed for self-definition on their own. We are introduced to them through exchanges with others who matter to us. . . . The genesis of the human mind is in this sense not "monological," not something each accomplishes on his or her own, but dialogical.[11]

This dialogical notion of the self is congruent with Gould's proposal that freedom entails social cooperation. Given the dialogical nature of the self, the development of the self could not be otherwise (except with great cost to the individual and society). In acknowledging the dialogic nature of the self, schools would provide multifaceted opportunities for students to interact with one another and with other adults at the school and in the community. Since we develop in a web of human relationships, it would make sense to think that the richer and more intricate that web, the more depth to our students' development.

The cultures within which one is situated play a large role in the growth and development of each of us. Our unique cultures provide the people, traditions, and history that allow us to interact dialogically. Culture provides the resources upon which we draw to create identities. Language carries the culture and the meanings that we make and, in that way, is an integral part of who we are. Attend to the critical role of language in creating meaning by reading the words of a Guatemalan refugee to this country who struggled to find voice and a place that would sustain his dignity:

> If we take into account that language is one of the most important aspects of man, as it is linked not only to his thoughts and

feelings but also to objective reality, logically, we are violating certain laws and categories that we recognize when we express ourselves in English. For a long time we sound like robots with no emotion, totally impersonal. This puts us in a situation of accommodation, resignation, and adjustment. These distressing circumstances lead to many difficulties and embarrassing moments which are irritating and isolating. Often, *we become eternally mute, being in a country which is still strange and feeling like distant spectators of the world.* (Emphasis mine)[12]

In this dramatic case, a struggle with a language itself created a sense of spectatorship and muteness. While many children come to our schools with such apparent language dilemmas, others come unprepared to draw upon the cultural resources of language. And perhaps in some schools, not realizing the significance of participating in language, we create students who are spectators. For example, when a child falls behind and struggles with reading, we strip down the reading program to worksheets and basal readers. In our attempt to get back to some basic skills, we remove the rich literary resources needed for development and engagement with learning. Too many times the richness of a culture is reserved for the brightest students, the gifted, those taking advanced placement classes. To confirm this, all one has to do is compare the syllabi of honors or gifted programs with those of remedial or basic programs. We must have a rich cultural context in order to define ourselves. If our cultural resources are sparse, then there are fewer chances to develop ourselves and our narratives suffer. Such resources must be extended to all students. It is not that all students learn alike or have the same academic abilities, but all students do need extensive and varied narrative resources through which they can develop themselves. To realize how this occurs, we must first describe the narrative nature of the self.

DIGNITY AND THE NARRATIVE NATURE OF THE SELF

Human beings are meaning makers, and, broadly speaking, a story is an expression of a person's attempt to make meaning. In *Acts of Meaning*, Jerome Bruner posits that human beings are "fueled by a need to construct a meaning."[13] We begin to experience the world from the first moment of life, and as we grow, we create meaning from the varied events of our lives and attribute significance to our compilation of experience. Is this not evident in the excitement of

a kindergarten class? Bruner's understanding illuminates the narrative nature of the self, as well as points to how the self is formed
interactively with culture. He says that the "self too must be treated
as a construction that, so to speak, proceeds from the outside in as
well as from the inside out, from culture to mind as well as from
mind to culture."[14] What opportunities are our students given in
school to facilitate the outward-in as well as the inside-out? Traditional education too often is concerned with the "filling up" of a
student, rather than paying attention to the interpretative and transformational aspects of learning.

The narrative, or story form, is a structure for making a life
coherent out of the conjure of life experience. Such coherence is
not to be found in the order of events that occur "out there" in a
life. Rather, as Rosenwald and Ochberg argue, "coherence derives
from the tacit assumptions of plausibility that shape the way each
story maker weaves the fragmentary episodes of experience into a
history."[15] The meaning or coherence we create contributes to the
developing sense of who we are. We have a history, a set of traditions,
meanings, and experiences, that provides a type of background against
which to measure ourselves.

This sense of self is not simply who we are by virtue of our role
definitions, but who we are at the protean core of ourselves. Here I
employ the term *protean core* to represent a self that remains aware of
its past and continuing identity, while acknowledging that it is ever
changing in its interactions with the world. Such a self finds expression in narrative form. This protean self, in turn, colors how we will
attribute meaning to past experience, as well as mediates how we will
understand new experience. Donald Polkinghorne develops this same
notion when he argues that the "self, then, is not a static thing or a
substance, but a configuring of personal events into an historical unity
which includes not only what one has been but also anticipations of
what one will be."[16] Embedded within a given context, the self develops from a mixture of things, among them temperament, relationships, and experience. Price and Simpkinson describe how this "mixture
of things" can come to form a narrative. They utilize Paul Tillich's
notion of "ultimate concern" as the "interior movement of our 'self'
in the unfolding of our lives." As we grapple with those things that
ultimately will create meaning in our lives, the self is moved. Although
this movement can appear linear in fashion, it rarely is. The self is
moved forward and back, around and around, as it responds to those
events that it encounters. Pushing this metaphor further, they state,

"That movement is driven by images. Often these images are linked to characters and events in our lives and are therefore narrated as stories. These stories, then, are tales of ultimate concern."[17] It is the continual movement of the self, driven by ultimate concern or meanings, that is captured in the narrative form of the core story.

Because the self is narrative in the way Bruner describes, we can imagine the narrativity of the self being expressed as story. We ache to say, "It happened to me in this way... " In *After Virtue*, Alasdair MacIntyre argues that since the self is storied, it becomes important to know the story within which one fits.[18] In other words, we must place our narrative within broader cultural narratives. From this we also gain meaning. Recall the Latino students in San Antonio whom Kohl visited. They had disengaged from schooling because they were being denied an opportunity to find the story within which they fit. When Kohl opened the door for them to enter with their story, then their education could begin. In our diverse cultural context, creating connections between one's own narrative and those of others would entail knowing many different stories. Because a child's daily life is, to a large extent, embedded in the context of schooling, education has a role to play in creating these connections. Hence, as I will discuss in chapter 7, education should be conceived as paying attention to stories in order to sustain and nurture children's dignity.

Even paying attention to relatively small matters in school can reflect our understanding of the protean and narrative nature of the self. Traditionally, school is "done" to us in a linear manner. We move year by year, grade by grade, teacher by teacher, along the lines of the factory model. But selves rarely develop so neatly. Children are not widgets, and something gets lost when one is passed from one grade to the next. Rather than follow this linear pattern that is not well matched to what we know about children's development, schools could provide multiage classrooms (not "splits") where student learning is not predefined by age groupings and where students can remain in relationships with the same adults and many of the same peers. This privileges the place of story in creating a life within the educational realm.

A SPACE FOR DIGNITY

In any discussion of dignity, it is crucial to understand that we cannot simply assume that dignity will develop and be sustained without any effort on our part to ensure it. It must be cultivated within a society and within a school. It is not enough to forego interfering with another's life. Nor is it enough to base a public ethic on a concern to prevent cruelty and humiliation, as Richard Rorty has suggested as a model for a postmodern ethic.[19] Rorty insists that "solidarity is not thought of as recognition of a core self, the human essence," but simply as a recognition that despite all our differences, we are similar in our desire to prevent pain, suffering, and humiliation. But Rorty's position does not get us far enough along, nor is it true to its own implicit understanding of human nature. While an ethic based on this notion of negative liberty may be effective in some spheres of political life, it does not provide enough guidance for how it is that lives can flourish. And I have argued earlier that adults involved in education must address the moral conditions under which children might flourish.

Although Rorty rejects the talk of dignity as foundationalist, he argues for the idea of redescription as a mode of moral discourse. Rather than arguing from a theological or foundationalist position, Rorty recommends that moral dialogue simply be a process of continuing redescription of what works for us as we are in the world, set against the background of preventing humiliation. In redescribing, we tell about the meaning of our lives, and as we bump up against one another, this meaning necessarily changes. This redescription expands our notion of "us" by showing the various stories of our lives.[20] Yet I argue that by utilizing dignity as a backdrop, we can still describe and redescribe in Rortyan fashion. While I hold constant the concept of dignity as a moral standard, how that dignity is implemented in the particularities of human lives and differing cultures remains interactive. Hence, Rorty reminds us that our language itself "determines what one can take as a possible project," and I point out that each culture will describe the range of projects for one's life differently.[21]

As I will argue in the next chapter, because the self is narrative in nature, we can sustain dignity through the use of stories. This strong link between sustaining dignity and sharing stories can guide our moral practice (including education) through a universal value and at the same time ground it in our human experience. This will prevent us from simply engaging in a Rortyan redescription ad infinitum, or conversely, from having no standard by which to measure the flourishing or dignity of lives. Dignity provides the backdrop or standard for the redescriptions. A standard that would not fall prey to the traditional critiques of foundationalism, and that would be culturally sensitive and inclusive, must be envisioned in a new way. To understand how dignity can fulfill this role, I employ Seyla Benhabib's post-Enlightenment notion of "interactive universalism," which she grounds on the following two principles: (1) universal moral respect, and (2) egalitarian reciprocity.[22] Identifying ways in which these two principles can be achieved is essential for the task of sustaining dignity. Paying attention to the stories that one tells is a way to achieve the two principles that Benhabib posits for our consideration. This is done in the following way.

The first principle of universal moral respect recognizes the "right of all beings capable of speech and action to be participants in the moral conversation."[23] In so stating, Benhabib endorses the need for a public conversation and a public space within which this can occur. In addition, participation must be inclusive of all who are able to make a contribution to the dialogue. Although Benhabib does not say it, in order to be inclusive, the heretofore acceptable modes of speech would have to be enlarged from where they are now. Currently, a very Western, logical, and analytic mode of speech predominates. Participation based upon this kind of speech has been challenged by underrepresented groups. In order to attain the principle of universal moral respect, the moral dialogue would have to be open to hearing other types of speech. Among others, one form of speech might be story.

The second principle of egalitarian reciprocity requires that within the moral conversation "each has the symmetrical rights to various speech acts, to initiate new topics."[24] Examining the interplay between story and dignity extends Benhabib's argument for these two principles by elaborating ways that the moral conversation can be inclusive and how egalitarian reciprocity can occur. It is one thing to state a need for such conversation and reciprocity and another to elaborate how this may be achieved. Stories and dignity speak specifically to the second principle in the following way. Paying attention to one another's stories is a fundamental way to create an egalitarian sense of reciprocity. Benhabib tells us what attaining such egalitarian reciprocity means. She argues that it is the "capacity to reverse perspectives, that is, the willingness to reason from the others' point of view, and the sensitivity to hear their voice is paramount."[25] Paying attention to stories speaks directly to how this reversal process might occur, and in creating reciprocity, universal moral respect is sustained. And as Benhabib and others argue, as more and more persons are allowed access to a public arena where discussions of dignity must be situated, then the particular meaning of dignity will change with the particularity of experience that each new person and culture brings to it. It will be a redescription of dignity for a certain time and place. In this way, Rorty is correct to say that there is an "indefinite plurality of standpoints" from which to tell the human story.[26] That notion in itself is indicative of dignity as it frames public discourse by requiring respect. But we must now return the discussion to the intersection of education and children's lives.

DIGNITY AND EDUCATION

The sense of reciprocity that Benhabib describes has implications for education. Our interest in dignity requires that we pay attention to the meaning and identity people are attempting to make in their lives since these are two of the central tasks of being human. While psycho-social marginalization is destructive of personal identity and meaning, hence an affront to dignity, paying attention to the meaning children are attempting to make in their lives enhances identity and a sense of dignity.[27] But, as previously noted, sustaining dignity is a relational and reciprocal activity. In the educational setting, reciprocity speaks to a need for mutual attentiveness to one another's stories.

In this regard, Vivian Paley describes how the preschool children in her class utilize their make-believe stories to accomplish certain things, such as conveying hidden meanings, establishing connections, revealing secret thoughts, and creating a sense of place and person. She indicates that while each child creates a discrete story, the process of that storytelling is not a private affair. She states: "Our kind of storytelling is a social phenomenon, intended to flow through all other activities and provide the widest opportunity for a communal response. Stories are not private affairs; the individual imagination plays host to all the stimulation in the environment and causes ripples of ideas to encircle the listeners."[28]

Because these stories are not private, and because they ripple through the audience, children are put in the position to be attentive to one another's narratives. If they choose not to attend to one another, then the ability to create a learning community is compromised. In addition, given the dialogical nature of the self, the ability to develop the self is likewise impacted. In the case of one little boy in Paley's classroom, Jason, and the story of his helicopter, it was the ultimate attentiveness to what his make-believe story meant for him that allowed him to connect with the other children and move forward in identity development and meaning making. Paley affirms the need for such attentiveness. She contends that "only by reaching into the endemic imagery of each child can we proceed together in any mutual enterprise. All else is superficial; we will not have touched one another."[29] This is the role of reciprocity. In giving mutual attention to one another, we acknowledge the relational context for sustaining dignity.

School represents a protected cultural space. It is not fully public, nor fully private. So rather than asking traditional questions, such as, What are the purposes of schooling? one might alternately ask, What can schools do in the lives of children? or, What could schools do to help children flourish? School is not quite a public space that would be characterized by fairly nonintimate and instrumental relationships, and it is not quite a private family space that would be characterized by intimate and nurturing relationships. So it is not the civil or political community at large; nor is it simply an extension of home.[30] Acknowledging this distinction is important in understanding what schools can do in the lives of their students. Two things schooling can do are, first, to reflect the narrative nature of the self as it develops and, second, to provide a place for students to come to know many different stories as well as articulate their own stories. Both endeavors sustain dignity and hence, the creation of lives.

Therefore, in order to sustain the dignity of children in our schools, we must respect them by paying attention to the meaning they are making in their lives. In my final chapter, I will describe in detail that paying attention to the meaning children are creating in their lives means (1) valuing their autonomy as "authors" of their lives, (2) encouraging reciprocity in relationships, (3) providing recognition rather than marginalization for the identity and meanings of selves, and (4) viewing education as encouraging the freedom to imagine. All these things speak to being concerned with the flourishing of children's lives, rather than protecting children's dignity through noninterference with the development of their lives.

Speaking of what it means to flourish, Eamonn Callan indicates that "(a)mong other things, to flourish as a person is to be capable of the fulfillment of human intimacy and solidarity, to be free to perfect one's talents, to be able to make independent choices about religious affiliation, vocation, and the like."[31] Upon reflection, we realize that flourishing speaks to something deeper about an individual, as does the notion of dignity. One way to come to know those "things that matter" that Taylor described earlier is through the sharing of our narrative selves, our stories, or the sense that we make of our lives.

How story can nurture and sustain dignity and lead to the flourishing of lives is where we now turn.

5

THE POWER OF STORY:
Identity Development and Meaning Making

THE NOTION OF CORE STORY

It will be helpful to begin with a consideration of the notion of story prior to discussing its characteristics. Recall from chapter 4 that human beings are meaning makers and that the development of the self and the coherence of a life are expressed narratively. Story is an oral or written narrative that carries psycho-social meaning, both individually and culturally. While a story grows out of the composite of a lived life, it clearly is more than just an ordering of objective facts about one's life. A story is a way for an individual to make sense of the objective "stuff" of life. A story is how individuals attach meaning or significance to the conjure of experience that fills their lives. I will refer to this as the telling of core stories, signifying stories that reveal the self and the meaning that one attaches to life experience, as opposed to chronological recitations of life events or a listing of roles one has. This notion of core stories stands in opposition to the type of story that simply reports on events without portending a self-given meaning. Rosenwald and Ochberg contribute to a more elaborate understanding of the import of stories that persons tell. They state:

> The stories people tell about themselves are interesting not only for the events and characters they describe but also for something in the construction of the stories themselves. How individuals recount their histories—what they emphasize and omit, their stance as protagonists or victims, the relationship the story establishes between the teller and audience—all shape what individuals can claim of their own lives. Personal stories are not merely a way of telling someone (or oneself) about one's life; they are the means by which identities may be fashioned.[1]

Stories that people tell are laden with meaning of the sorts that Rosenwald and Ochberg point to. Stories and, more specifically, the telling of them contribute to the identity development of the individual. Stories, then, play an integral role in sustaining and nurturing dignity, given that dignity must accord respect to the development of lives.

Generated from her work with children's own stories, Vivian Paley notes the uniqueness of a meaningful story and states that "none of us [is] to be found in sets of tasks or lists of attributes; we can be known only in the unfolding of our unique stories within the context of everyday events."[2] So even though stories sometimes can appear seemingly full of insignificant happenings, they can be core stories as they reveal the self and permit one the opportunity to be known by another. In his autobiography, Richard Rodriguez explains how this telling of one's story serves to reveal. He states, "Such is the benefit of language: By finding public words to describe one's feelings, one can describe oneself to oneself. One names what was previously only darkly felt."[3] Therefore, core stories are to be differentiated from stories that simply chronicle a list of facts about one's life. Core stories convey the meaning of our unique selves.

Given the central tasks of development, paying attention to core stories is one way to ascertain the meaning children are creating in their lives. For the purposes of this work, I will make a distinction between core stories and traditional story form. It is helpful to make this distinction because traditional story form may or may not carry significant meaning. For example, a story told in typical form may be a travelogue of a summer vacation listing dates, places, and events without speaking to the meaning of those events in an individual's life. Conversely, the meaning an individual may attempt to convey may not be in the literal form of a story. Utilizing the notion of core story allows us to pay attention to the meaning and identity one is creating in his or her life and acknowledges that such meaning is usually conveyed in a narrative form; hence, the use of story is in contrast to other forms of conveying information, such as the argument. When I speak of core story, I speak of the meaning an individual is attempting to form or articulate, whether or not it is framed in the traditional form of a story.

In schools, core stories may or may not reside in the traditional story form. Making biographical or chronological lists describing the self at the beginning of the school year does little to reveal the meaning or sense that students make in their lives. Providing more open-ended and narrative spaces for writing or responding to interesting questions may. For example, one teacher has students draw themselves on the cover of *Time* magazine as the Person or Student of the Year and then write a page about why they received this honor. These hand-drawn covers of *Time* magazine then adorn the walls as a reminder of who it is that resides in this classroom and perhaps gives us a glimpse into what meaning and even dreams these young people have in their lives.

But stories are not only written, or accessed in such planned activities. Many times the sense that children are making of their lives is revealed in their informal conversations, or if teachers are lucky, it is found serendipitously through their classroom study, during breaks, at recess, responding to stories read aloud. While there is great variety in when, where, and how these meanings can be revealed, what these all have in common is that there must be places or spaces created for this meaning to emerge. Instead of always "filling up" the curriculum, teachers may look for places to "open up." This is critical because as John Dewey indicated:

> Enforced quiet and acquiescence prevent pupils from disclosing their real natures. They enforce artificial uniformity. *They put seeming before being.* They place a premium upon preserving the outward appearance of attention, decorum, and obedience. And everyone who is acquainted with schools in which this system prevailed well knows that thoughts, imaginations, desires, and sly activities ran their own unchecked course behind this facade. They were disclosed to the teacher only when some untoward act led to their detection. (Emphasis mine)[4]

Dewey's critique of the traditional model of schooling points out that uniformity of schooling separates the child from having educative experiences. The thoughts, imaginations, and desires of the students are kept hidden from the teacher, and when this occurs, significant learning cannot occur because learning must access these very spots of meaning making. Without teachers actively looking for places where students can bring their "real natures" to the task of learning, Dewey goes on to say that "there is only an accidental chance that the material of study and the methods used in instruction will so come home to an individual that his development of mind and character is actually directed." Hence, without paying attention to the manner in which children create meaning, schooling fails to be educative. Whether formal or informal, story is a significant carrier and site of meaning making.

STORY AND THE FLOURISHING OF LIVES

Story can be more than just an enjoyable yarn that is spun around the campfire. Rather, story can help address the Aristotelian question of How should a human being live? It is this question that underlies the concern for dignity in the process of education. It asks us to consider what it means for lives of children to *flourish*. Two ways to answer such a question are either by making a list of psychological characteristics or by analytically describing what flourishing might mean. But story offers us another and more appropriate avenue toward understanding dignity and the flourishing of lives. The work of Martha Nussbaum reveals how the particular nature of story is commensurate to describing the unique nature of the human condition. She indicates that "certain literary texts are indispensable to a philosophical inquiry in the ethical sphere: not by any means sufficient, but sources of insight without which the inquiry cannot be complete."[5] Because we are rooted in our particularity, we must turn to sources that provide accounts of this particularity. Nussbaum argues that the carrier of much of this knowledge is found in the forms of fictional, storied work. In other words, story is a mode befitting our inquiry about the human condition.

Applied to our discussion, story provides a means for articulating what it might mean for children to flourish. In addition, as argued earlier, story is constitutive of personal identity because personal identity is formed by creating a sense of narrative unity. Paying attention to children's stories sustains and nurtures their dignity as it acknowledges the central tasks of development, that is, the creation of meaning and identity. In doing so, it counteracts the tendency toward psycho-social marginalization. Story, as an expression of the narrative coherence of the self, provides the vehicle for meaning and identity to be articulated.

Let me add one more point about paying attention. On its surface, the task of paying attention refers to the adults entrusted with the care of children. But, additionally, there is a task for children who learn from the example of their teacher. One of the roles of the teacher would then be to attend to the child's story in order that the child might learn to do the same for her or himself and for others in the classroom. This is a powerful point that relates to the sustaining of personal dignity. I said at the outset that although it is difficult, personal dignity could be sustained through self-ascription. Yet in order for this to occur, the child needs to have caring adults help him or her learn how to do this. Since paying attention to story as the carrier of meaning and identity sustains dignity, it is critical that the child learn to pay attention to his or her own story and how it fits in with the larger social constructions of his or her world.[6]

Further, thinking about stories in this sense has the powerful potential to nurture and sustain dignity in ways that encompass both the private and the public realm. Within personal experience, stories have the potential to create identity and forge connections between persons. I will speak to the means of creating connections in my next chapter. But in addition to this, within a more public realm, stories have the power to sustain dignity by opening the public conversation for all to become party to culturally negotiated meaning. This occurs in the following way.

In chapter 4, I made reference to Benhabib's argument that in order to ground a certain sense of universalism, one needed to employ two principles. These were (1) universal moral respect, and (2) egalitarian reciprocity. These two principles lay the groundwork for expanding the public conversation by requiring what Benhabib describes as a "capacity to reverse perspectives . . . the willingness to reason from the others' point of view, and the sensitivity to hear their voice."[7] Story provides the avenue to attain these three skills, and coupled with the first principle of moral respect that allows all voices to be heard, many more voices can be added to a public dialogue about things that matter. Whether we like how the added voices change the dialogue or how much the conversation really changes are not the issues at stake here. What is certain is that as the public dialogue becomes more inclusive, of necessity it changes by virtue of the additional perspectives and stories. That change may be rapid or painfully slow, but it will impact the dialogue. Whether and where this public dialogue may or may not be taking place today is a matter of debate which is outside the scope of this work to address. It is a crucial question that must be addressed. But in the ways described above, story fits the particular domain of schooling, which is a blend of the private and public. Others have written of how the capacity, willingness, and sensitivity to other perspectives might be facilitated in schools. Activities such as role playing and drama allow students to try on perspectives other than their own. Milbrey McLaughlin and colleagues have worked with diverse groups of young people in urban settings, having them write and then trade dramatic dialogues so that each has voice, and then each must "try on" the voice of the other.[8]

The domain of schooling has the potential to be a space where rich dialogue can take place because generally it is a space small enough that individual lives can matter. It is not necessary for abstract ethical, political, psychological, or policy principles to override the need to pay attention to the individual development of lives. Providing a focus on contextuality and paying attention to individual lives and their dignity have been part of the works of Gilligan, Noddings, and Martin, who take seriously the notion of contextuality and who introduce the ethic of care to the discourse on morality.[9] Adults and children are immersed in the context of human relationships throughout the school day. Accepting the ethic of care as a moral position enriches our understanding of how human beings relate to one another and enhances our understanding of dignity by paying attention to the individual in context, rather than calling upon disembodied ethical principles to guide our conduct.

Yet such considerations of caring fall short of making essential connections with dignity. For example, when adults in schools care so much about children's ability to learn that they devise a system of evaluation in order to provide special services, but then the system itself harms children, we are lacking an essential connection between care and dignity. In such instances, it is assumed that the adults care about the children, but the way in which assessments are done, labels are attached, and services delivered must continually be measured against the backdrop of a student's dignity. When we do not measure our efforts against this backdrop, marginalization can occur. Lacking such connections, we are left to wonder more specifically about the nature of the ways we care and how caring might nurture dignity and how it counteracts forces that marginalize.

One way we may understand the ethic of care and its role in the preservation of dignity is by paying attention to the stories of others that encompass the particulars of their lives.

When our human relationships at school are governed by rules and we treat everyone the same under the guise of fairness, we are at the same time conveying the message to students that the particulars of their lives do not count for much. As educators, we are concerned that students grow into responsible citizens. We ask them to be accountable for their actions, but we set up a false dichotomy if we act as though the only choice is between rule-governed schools that treat everyone as if they were the same or schools that play favorites, have elite student and parent groups, and may not require students to be responsible for their choices. Is there not a difference between the student who chooses to skip school for the fun of it and the student who does not attend because she worked a shift job into the wee hours of the morning to help provide financial support for her mother and siblings? If they are both to be suspended under the rules of the school, then the school has chosen to ignore the particulars of lives and in so doing marginalizes the meaning making of the students and puts truly educative experiences at risk. Educative experience requires accessing the space for core stories.

DEFINING CHARACTERISTICS OF CORE STORIES

Let us consider some characteristics that are necessary to our identifying and understanding the power of core stories. A core story encompasses a way of telling about one's life that possesses the following defining characteristics.

(1) A core story provides a coherence of meaning to an individual's life experience. It reveals one's sense of continuity by creating a coherent notion of the self. The self with such a story understands that it is him or herself that persists through time and claims authorship of a given story with its attendant meaning. It is the storied self as Rosenwald and Ochberg describe, "This person I am today is who I have been years becoming."[10] While ascription of meaning changes over time, the individual maintains a more or less coherent sense of the self within a given context. One does not experience the disjointedness of wondering who one was yesterday or worry about who one might be tomorrow. Rather, one gains coherence as one ascribes meaning to the continual flux of experience.

Although coherence implies a singular self, as I discussed in chapter 4, creating one's story is not a solitary endeavor. While the self should be seen as the "primary" author of its own story, the family and cultural milieu serves as the interactive setting for development of such a story. Noting the significance of the social context, Brody proposes that "the primary human mechanism for attaching meaning to particular experiences is to tell stories about them. Stories serve to relate individual experiences to the explanatory constructs of the society and culture and also to place the experiences within the context of a particular individual's life history."[11]

This coherence is created by virtue of commonalties of experience that occur within a given family, community, culture, and history. Eva Hoffman describes how this occurs. She authors her life story, *Lost in Translation,* and comments that "meaning is interhuman and comes from the thickness of human connections and how richly you are known."[12] Being known to others creates this thickness of human connections. While the connections of language and culture constitute how we shape our meaning, it is the individual who lays claim to his or her own experiences as his or her own story. Culture constrains but does not determine what story we create by way of experience. I will return to this point in the next chapter.

There is also a coherence to story that occurs due to a sense of the self that persists through time. While sense of self may become fragile at times, the self generally does persist through time and creates a continuity in the telling of the story. Brody explains it thus:

> Personal identity must be assumed if the narrative is to be that of one life; but at the same time, what establishes the identity relation between the person at time t-1 and the same person at time t-2 . . . is the fact that the narrative of the lives of both persons is the selfsame narrative. One's action is truly one's own, for which one is responsible, because it appears in the narrative of one's life in an intelligible manner. The narrative serves to explain the connectedness of that action with one's other actions, motives, and desires.[13]

As one ascribes meaning to these experiences, they are temporally tied together. There is a continuing sense that the experiences of my past belong to me in the same way the experiences I anticipate in the future will belong to me. This continuing or temporal sense of the self and meaning can be facilitated in schools as students and teachers spend an extended time with each other. Rather than changing teachers and classes every year or semester, some schools are trying out different methods of providing this continuity. Students may be in a two- or three-year multiaged classroom, where they remain with the same teacher. Others are creating teams of teachers that stay with a smaller group or team of middle or high school students as they progress through the grades. An elementary school is sending a teacher through all the grades with one particular class, and when they graduate, the teacher will accept a new class of students with whom she or he will spend perhaps six years of educating.

(2) A core story represents a fiction of sorts, rather than a description of fact. When we speak of meaning, we are not necessarily speaking of facts. Some may question whether stories must represent historical fact. While there must be a general sense of coherence in order to create a shared past that is recognizable to the appropriately involved individuals, many times the stories that give meaning for us are not based on agreed historical facts. This occurs most noticeably within family relationships. The same experience is construed differently, or, in retrospect, what one thinks was the same experience is remembered in very different ways based upon the meanings each individual bestows upon the set of events.

But because story does not necessarily represent factual happenings, the importance of the meaning the individual has created is not negated. On the contrary, the meaning each individual gives to his or her experience should be heard and acknowledged. That meaning may appear flawed or may not agree with our own interpretation, but until the individual who is attempting to convey meaning has the experience of being understood, there is no potential for the meaning that the individual carries to change.

Let me provide an example that speaks to this point. In *The Call of Stories,* Robert Coles tells a story that demonstrates the importance of attending to personal meaning in human relationships.[14] As a new resident assigned to the psychiatric unit of Massachusetts General Hospital, Coles was both excited and nervous at the same time. He was given the names of his new patients. Of course, as with any new psychiatric resident, he was to be supervised by those who were older and more experienced than he. He had two such supervisors: Dr. Binger and Dr. Ludwig. During their weekly supervision meetings, Dr. Binger strove to build the confidence of his new resident by emphasizing the importance of a thorough understanding and application of psychiatric theory. Dr. Ludwig, who was considered a little "over-the-hill" and hard-of-hearing, took another approach. Making little headway using traditional psychiatric theory with a particularly difficult, "phobic" patient, Coles met with Dr. Ludwig. Dr. Ludwig began by telling him a story about a former patient, about the details of her life and experience. Then he stopped. He did not impersonalize the story by calling it a clinical history, nor did he amplify it by placing the proper theoretical terms in just the right spots. Rather, referring to the patient in the story, he asked Coles, "Do you see her in your mind?" And, of course, Coles did. That question stimulated a new way for Coles to understand and connect with his patients. Dr. Ludwig concluded that day's supervision by stating, "The people who come to see us bring us their stories. They hope they tell them well enough so that we understand the truth of their lives. They hope we know how to interpret their stories correctly. We have to remember that what we hear is *their story*." Gaining courage, Coles ventured out and attempted to reach this difficult patient with whom he had had no luck. After an awkward beginning, and surprising even himself, he simply asked this woman, "Why don't you just tell me a story or two?" From that point on, gradually, the leaves of her story unfolded. Coles was able to "understand the palpable pain and suffering of another human being," and this woman, with her heretofore driven and phobic behavior, was able to relax and share the meaning of her life with another. He happened to be her psychiatrist.

Dr. Ludwig's wise advice reminded Coles that each human being brings his or her story to us, and it is advice that educators likewise must heed if they hope to be effective teachers. My account of dignity asks each of us to recognize that each child who crosses our paths in schools brings his or her unique story. Not only that, but as Ludwig illuminated, "They hope they tell them well enough so that we understand the truth of their lives. They hope we know how to interpret their stories correctly." Children bring hope into the classroom that we will be perceptive enough not to miss their stories.

Does the emphasis on the importance of individual meaning require that we throw all standards of judgment out the window and treat every narrative as equal? The answer is both yes and no. Ethically and psychologically, if we are to meet the other, we must first understand his or her construal of meaning regardless of whether we find it accurate or reasonable. If this is our primary concern (and Coles' experience suggests that it might be fundamental to making other judgments), then yes, each narrative is to be seen as equal to

another. But, historically, if we are interested in making valid knowledge claims and ethical judgments, then standards of judging narratives are appropriate. They certainly would not look like the standards
for scientific validity, for example. They would have their own standards of judgment, just as scientific inquiry does.[15]

Even in cases of making medical, psychological, or educational
judgments, standards are necessary. But what is often overlooked is
the ethical responsibility first to understand the meaning of the
narrative and then allow that meaning to inform one's judgment.
For example, I recall a young third-grade girl who stole small items
from her teacher's purse. Knowing only the facts of this case, that
the girl actually stole items, would do little to understand or help
this child. This child would simply be punished or suspended from
school. Perhaps from an institutional or legal perspective, she should.
Yet understanding the possible meaning of *why* she did these acts
might lead one to make a different judgment. This child displayed
the symptoms of fetal alcohol syndrome. She lived with her father in
a motel on the local highway strip. Her mother had deserted her
early in life. This motherless young child was stealing things such as
pretty little mirrors, hair clips, and so on from her female teacher.
She was trying to find a mother's influence. Did this teacher "turn
her in"? Report her to the authorities? No. Instead she drew closer
to the child, talked with her, and let her know that if she needed any
of those things, she could come and ask her. It is crucial to determine the meaning by which the individual understands the experience before judgment can be made in an educative sense. Not only
might it change our judgment regarding the individual, but understanding another's meaning which is different than our own possible
construal might change us. Coherence, the first characteristic of
story, is, in part, the creation of a system of meaning; and meaning
is not burdened by historical fact.

(3) *Core stories have the unique capacity to deal with all the experiences
of our lives.* Especially and uniquely so, core stories can accommodate
the ambiguities, contradictions, and breaks in meaning that occur in
a life. On the one hand, stories are a record of how we place meaning on the experiences of our lives. Yet on the other hand, stories have
the unique capacity to acknowledge and accept the ambiguities and
contradictions that our life experience engenders. Creating and having a story is a uniquely phenomenological experience; it is telling
how experience happens for oneself. As noted in the first condition,

having a story presupposes that the self is experienced as a unifying entity. As an example, in *Stories of Sickness*, Brody, drawing from the field of medicine, demonstrates how sickness can be understood as having a break in one's story, rather than having a particular pathological condition. Hence the person who experiences cancer does not simply have a disease that ravages the body, but also has an experience that ravages his or her life. Brody rejects Cartesian dualism and embraces a phenomenological perspective of the person as a unified whole. This notion can be expanded usefully from the context of sickness and applied to those events that cause us to rethink or renegotiate the meaning of our experiences. So when events occur that fall outside the realm of typical explanation, we experience a "disruption of self—an unpleasantly experienced break or split in a sense of personhood that ought, instead, to be felt as whole or complete."[16] How can our stories encompass such disruptions?

What is unique to stories is that they have a place for such disruptions, ambiguities, and contradictions in a way that perhaps no other way of making sense does. For instance, Thomas Kuhn has argued that the scientific community does not deal with contradictory evidence or ambiguities. Rather, they attribute the anomalies of research to a flaw in the investigator or scientific procedure.[17] Likewise, in the world of institutions and bureaucracies, certainly there is little or no room for those events that fall outside of the expected. "Sorry, but I have to follow the rules," is the standard refrain we hear when we try to present our unique and contextual experience to bureaucratic ears. Though the major religions each have an important role for story, they commonly appear to have decided in advance and by tradition which questions, paradoxes, or disruptions they will tolerate and which will not be part of their dogma.

One of the great draws of the story then is that it allows the complexities of human nature and the inexplicable contingencies of life. Story does not pretend to have the answer for everything. Rather, story can accommodate experiences in life that may not quite make sense to a person, as well as encompassing those experiences that do. For example, Paley indicates that for one child in her room at the Chicago Lab School, stories provide room for such confusion. She states, "There are no certainties and no answers. Joseph has envisioned a story in which to place his confusion. Having told his story and acted it out, he knows something he did not know before."[18] Stories make room for all our experiences and allow them to season for a while before finding a place to settle in our system of meaning.

And in some cases, perhaps they remain forever on the periphery. Stories have the capacity to accommodate such ambiguity.

(4) Core stories allow the teller to determine what is pertinent. The story is told in the voice of the teller. Given that each of our stories is influenced by and reflects multiple voices in our past, a core story still reflects that which the teller ascertains as pertinent. Empowering the teller of stories goes to the heart of why stories underwrite dignity. They are an acknowledgment of the voice and an assignment of pertinence by the teller, whether or not the story may seem rational, sensible, or even likely. For example, if you were to tell me in all earnestness that unbeknownst to me, you were really a Martian, I would have to pay attention to your claim. I would have to decide whether you were pulling my leg or using this as a heuristic strategy or were completely serious. From that point, I then determine a course of action. But what is significant is that I am paying attention to a meaning that you feel is significant, even if it seems beyond the bounds of belief to me. This differs from the realm of science where the pertinency of questions may be dictated by the theory itself and the contemporary scientific community, the members of which do not talk of extraterrestials! Additionally, one hopes that the stories of meaning that children bring to us in the schools will not seem as alien!

The narrative voice that assigns pertinency does so by virtue of its unique standing as author of the story. The teller of the story is both observer of past action and present interpreter of events. Brody makes the distinction that this narrative voice is both distant and intimate at the same time. He states:

> Distance exists because the narrator is separated from the narrated events in time and thus can assume a reflective, observant posture toward those events in a way that was impossible when the events were in progress. Intimacy exists, . . . because the narrator *is* the individual mentioned in the narrative, is responsible for the events disclosed, and thus has a personal stake in how others react to the telling of the story.[19]

Core stories have the special capability of allowing the teller to be both principal and narrator, observed and observer. It is this dual role that provides the opportunity for stories to change even the teller of the story. As one steps out of the story and acts as narrator, one gains a distance that may allow for insight, judgment, and reflection. In my own life, I have had many experiences where I have gained an insight simply through articulating my story to someone else. In saying it aloud, I saw heretofore invisible connections, and in many cases, I gained a new appreciation for the perspective of others who were in my story, perhaps even as adversaries. As Wiersma describes it, "we discover the snags, inconsistencies, murkiness, or even downright surprises in our thoughts when we put them into words."[20] This is one of the educational reasons for asking students to keep journals. The educative experience does not come with the teacher's assessment of the journal, but in the actual process of thinking, reflecting, and writing, one creates meaning through these actions. Students often will say, "You know, I never saw that connection before!"

(5) *Core stories allow one to render public one's experience.* Building upon the characteristics of authorship and pertinency, telling one's story is often an important public endeavor for the storyteller in particular. Telling his own life story in *Hunger of Memory*, Richard Rodriguez notes the power of language and story to accomplish this. He affirms:

> For by rendering feelings in words that a stranger can understand—words that belong to the public, this Other—the young diarist no longer need feel all alone or eccentric. His feelings are capable of public intelligibility. In turn, the act of revelation helps the writer better understand his own feelings. Such is the power of language: By finding public words to describe one's feelings, one can describe oneself to oneself. One names what was previously only darkly felt.[21]

This ability to describe oneself, out loud as it were, reveals oneself to oneself and to a possible audience. In accomplishing this, dignity is affirmed as the unique nature of the self is acknowledged in a public forum.

This public sharing of the self has psychological consequences. It is a social act that counteracts anonymity. Paley confirms this process: "Our kind of storytelling is a social phenomenon, intended to flow through all other activities and provide the widest opportunity for a communal response. Stories are not private affairs; the individual imagination plays host to all the stimulation in the environment and causes ripples of ideas to encircle the listeners."[22] When stories are shared in this public way, although they are intensely personal and private, they have the capacity to have an enormous public impact as listeners respond. Additionally, there accrues a psychological and emotional efficacy in simply telling, beyond what a possible public response could provide. Sometimes a story must first be told to a more or less anonymous public, rather than shared with intimate others. This is what Rodriguez suggests when he says, "From such an intimate one must sometimes escape to the company of strangers, . . . in order to form new versions of oneself."[23] And, after all, forming new versions of ourselves is part of the task of identity making. Schooling, as it is situated between the public and private, is an appropriate place to try this out where the costs of trying and failing should not be so high as to prevent this kind of educational risk taking.

(6) *Core stories have the potential to counteract cultural givens that may otherwise dominate our lives.* This characteristic follows from making one's story public. It is story that allows us to challenge the strictures of culture. Rosenwald and Ochberg describe how narrative pushes the edge of cultural "circumscription of discourse." They state:

> It is possible, though surely difficult, to enlarge the range of personal narrative. Individuals and communities may become aware of the political-cultural conditions that have led to the circumscription of discourse. If a critique of these conditions occurs widely, it may alter not only how individuals construe their own identities but also how they talk to one another and indirectly the social order itself. Discourse mediates between the fate of the individual and the larger order of things.[24]

Rosenwald and Ochberg suggest that this pushing of the edges of culture occurs because narrative is always tempered by desire. Our desires, while informed by culture, also challenge culture. Rosenwald and Ochberg argue that though culture shapes who we are to a large extent, we also bring our human nature with its attendant desires to culture. These natural desires push at the edges of culture. They also argue that "Human nature, the materiality of life, is not reducible to time-bound local forms that culture offers it. It seeks forever to escape these forms.[25] This explains, in part, how the hermeneutic circle of human experience and narrative is not doomed by its own closure.

Education, in its richest sense, is based on the assumption that there is something about the human spirit that can rise above its social enculturation. If this were not the case, we would never escape forms of domination and discrimination because we would simply accept our society's message regarding the correct form of social relations. Yet as humans we look for, hope for, yearn for something more or that which is beyond the bounds of culture, all the while being defined by it. This paradox is central to being human. Education that facilitates this kind of growth and freedom is rarely incorporated into our national or state standards. Rene Arcilla suggests that education can engage even our adolescent "misanthropes" as it asks the questions that go to the core of meaning. He suggests that an education that is concerned with meaning

> takes the very questions which drive adolescents away from a society of hypocritical answers and tropes them so that they instead initiate adolescents into the uncertain vulnerability that marks our lives in common. In this fashion, it recovers the central role that questioning, rather than argument, had in the Socratic response to the sophists; it reaffirms a treasure of philosophy's childhood. Philosophy is thus the name of a discourse in which the sincerely unsure . . . find each other. It is the kind of discourse that promises to help you talk with, and not just to, the misanthropic student.[26]

These are the spaces where peoples around the world and through time have centered their stories and myths that focus on meaning making. Education, at its best, interrogates those structures, beliefs, and relationships that define what it means to be human and holds discourse about those that oppress or hinder.

In *Domination and the Arts of Resistance*, James Scott argues that domination represents a power relationship that creates both public and hidden transcripts. The public transcript is the story of the dominant in a given culture, and the hidden transcript is that which lies outside of the hegemonic influence. Recall in chapter 3 how Scott described the hidden transcript as the "privileged site for nonhegemonic, contrapuntl [sic], dissident, subversive discourse."[27] It is where something other than the dominant story can be told. When breaks in the public transcript occur, the hidden transcript rises and challenges the cultural givens. Whereas domination creates a "fragmentation of discourse," making a space for the hidden transcript to be heard creates a greater inclusivity for the culture. Rather than explicating the relationship between domination and material exploitation, Scott focuses on how domination affects dignity and autonomy. In the same way, I focus on psycho-social marginalization that impacts dignity, rather than on stereotypic marginalization. Neither material exploitation or stereotypic marginalization is an ethically acceptable form of human relationship, but this work is addressing the more insidious threats to the dignity of the self.

With this focus on dignity, the notion of sharing stories as a means of overcoming marginalizing cultural givens becomes cogent. Sharing core stories becomes a way of gaining recognition for how one experiences a life. Bruner claims that "to be in a viable culture is to be bound in a set of connecting stories, connecting even though the stories may not represent a consensus."[28] In telling one's story, one becomes a party to negotiating public and cultural givens and as one's voice and story are affirmed, one's dignity is enhanced through public acknowledgment of one's story.

How many times do we ask our students and our children, "What is school like for you?" "How do you like how I'm teaching this topic?" "What is it like on the playground?" Do we invite student voices into the public space of school? The consequence of inviting these stories into the public space of schooling is that how we "do" education might change; that is, if we take their responses seriously. It is this possibility or potential for change itself that allows us to become a part of creating a reciprocal learning community. When the possibility that my "voice" might change the community is non-existent, then no learning community can exist. It shuts off the possibility of growth, and that is antithetical to what it means to be part of a *learning* community.

(7) Core stories are protean due to the contextual and relational nature of the self. One's story does not stay the same over time, nor does the self that the story reflects. Experience generated from both internal and external sources erodes and enhances the meaning an individual posits and, in such interactions, changes the meaning we attach to our particular lives. In addition, we greet each day with our current understandings, but we also create meaning retrospectively when we compile our experiences and attempt to make sense of them. Bruner argues as well for understanding the changing nature of the self due to its capacity for reflexivity. He describes this as "our capacity to turn around on the past and alter the present in its light,

or to alter the past in the light of the present. Neither the past nor the present stays fixed in the face of this reflexivity. The 'immense repository' of our past encounters may be rendered salient in different ways as we review them reflexively, or may be changed by reconceptualization."[29] Hence, the changing nature of one's story points to the changing nature of the self. Stories change because the self changes, and the self changes as do the stories. In this way, stories are both transformational and open to transformation. Wiersma's argument supports my claim. She states that stories should be considered "not only expressive but formative as well." Interestingly enough, she indicates that it is the ambiguity inherent to story that permits the interplay between story and action to be transformative.[30]

In summary, I have identified the defining characteristics of core stories as those characteristics that are necessary for understanding the power stories have in preserving dignity and overcoming forces that marginalize. These are *first*, that stories provide a coherence and meaning to individual experience; *second*, that core stories represent a fiction of sorts, rather than historical fact; *third*, that they have a unique capacity to deal with our life experience, especially with ambiguities, contradictions, and breaks in the meaning of one's experience; *fourth*, that the teller of the story must decide what is pertinent and tell the story in her or his own voice; *fifth*, that core stories enable one to render public one's experience; *sixth*, that they create the possibility of counteracting cultural givens that may dominate one's life and those of others; and *seventh*, that core stories are ever protean and transformational as life experience changes and the individual develops. I am aware that each of these characteristics represents complex human activities and cannot be as easily categorized as the written word makes it appear. In life experience, one characteristic and its ensuing activity may overlap with another until they appear indistinguishable. The value of articulating each characteristic on its own is that it provides a glimpse into the moral and psychological complexity of the role of core stories in human life.

In the next chapter, I will address the relationship between dignity and story and what moral responsibilities derive from this relationship.

6

Story and Our Moral Responsibility:
Tellers and Listeners

The Moral Responsibility of Storytelling

Story is relational and reciprocal and, as such, entails moral responsibilities. As we tell stories and listen to stories, we stand in a moral relation to one another. The process itself is reciprocal, that is, I tell a story and you listen, and then you tell a story and I listen. But the notion of reciprocity extends beyond this. Reciprocity does not simply mean that we share stories back and forth, but that we have an obligation to listen and tell in ways that will sustain the dignity of one another and avoid domination. In fact, Adam Zachary Newton describes how story actually forms an ethical encounter. Speaking of stories, he states:

> Cutting athwart the mediatory role of reason, narrative situations create an immediacy and force, framing relations of provocation, call, and response that bind narrator and listener, author and character, or reader and text. Again, these relations will often precede decision and understanding, with consciousness arriving late, after the assumption or imposition of intersubjective ties. . . . Stories, like persons, originate alogically.[1]

This chapter will examine how dignity can be sustained by paying attention to story. It is accomplished in two ways. Paying attention to core stories sustains dignity, first, by creating connections between persons, and, second, by naming that which dominates/marginalizes, as well as that which enhances and sustains dignity.

As with any powerful human activity, there is a potential for harm as well as good. In this regard, I will discuss how stories may be dominated by others, as well as how story can be used to dominate. The consequence of these forms of domination is that the meaning individuals are attempting to convey becomes invisible. This domination occurs through interference with one's story, usurpation of meaning, prepackaging of meaning, superficiality, and a neglect of contextuality. These will be discussed later in this chapter. What all these forms of domination have in common is that the right to author one's life is compromised.

STORIES AND DIGNITY

I turn now to a discussion of ways in which stories preserve dignity, both personal dignity, and relational dignity, previously discussed in chapter 4. In one sense, dignity cannot be destroyed because it is a characteristic of one's humanness. But understanding dignity in this way alone does not do justice to the importance of the role of others in nurturing and sustaining dignity. Recall my discussion in chapter 4 of the dialogical nature of the self. Precisely because we are embedded within social contexts from the moment of our birth, we also must pay attention to the social realm where dignity may be diminished or enhanced. Given the defining characteristics of core stories, thinking about persons as having stories has the powerful potential to enhance and sustain human dignity in ways that encompass both the personal and the relational realm. Let us explore how this occurs.

The first point I wish to make is that stories have a powerful potential to create connections between persons. These connections are important to achieving dignity in its richest sense. Dignity will be preserved when connections between persons are made that are noninstrumental in nature. To understand the importance of the distinction between instrumental and noninstrumental uses, we can imagine an example of a relationship that is instrumental in nature to understand how that type of relationship cannot sustain dignity. If a teacher cares about a student only as that student can either further or reflect the teacher's own professional work and success, then ultimately the connection will fail because the relationship is all about only one person's life, that is, the teacher's. When a relationship has no reciprocity, then the dignity of the student cannot be sustained because the individual's potential to create one's own unique life is not recognized. While it may appear as feigned interest, the dignity-sustaining nature of the relationship ultimately will fail when the demands of the student's life impinge on the work of the teacher. If the teacher were interested in this student's life in a noninstrumental way, then the teacher would be interested in knowing what life was like for this person and how he or she could assist appropriately in the development of that life. Story is a vehicle for conveying that meaning. Education, in a noninstrumental fashion, would start with a consideration of the student's life, rather than imposing on the student an externally defined curriculum. Another way to articulate this is to say that only if persons are perceived in a Kantian fashion as ends in themselves and not merely as means to another, can dignity be sustained.

To create a connection that is noninstrumental in nature so that dignity is sustained, the authenticity of each person must be recognized. Developing connections with others that sustain dignity must take the notion of authenticity into account. What might this mean? Recall the notion of authenticity in chapter 4 set forth by Taylor that speaks to creating a life that is uniquely "my own." He elaborates further:

> [Authenticity] accords crucial moral importance to a kind of contact with myself, with my own inner nature, which it sees as in danger of being lost, partly through the pressures of outward conformity. . . . Being true to myself means being true to my own originality, and that is something only I can articulate and discover. In articulating it, I am also defining myself. I am realizing a potentiality that is properly my own. This is the background understanding to the modern ideal of authenticity.[2]

Respect for the voice and the development of each individual must be given in order to ensure authenticity and hence dignity, and in this respect, stories become the vehicle for that voice. As I argued in chapter 4, authorship and authenticity are complementary. By paying attention to another's core story, I can create a noninstrumental, authentic connection between that person and myself.

It works in this way. You, who have heretofore been a stranger or an "other" to me, become a little more known to me by virtue of the story you tell. We may share small threads of commonalties. Perhaps you are a mother, as am I; perhaps you are a musician and so speak a language I understand. Perhaps you have felt a grievous loss, and I, too, understand such pain. As you reveal yourself to me, two things occur. The first is that I will find some commonalties that illuminate our sameness. At the same time, a second thing occurs. Even if there is little we share, you are affirming your dignity as you tell your story. You have caught my attention as you say, "Here I am. This is my experience." This affirms your dignity as you and I carve out a space to articulate the meaning of your experience. While this expression demonstrates your personal dignity, the full sense of dignity will be realized when the listener acknowledges you and your story.

Additionally, stories create connections through their ability to reveal one's understandings and values by illuminating how one ascribes meaning to experience. The telling of core stories allows the hearer to know the teller in a way that goes beyond knowing that person by the roles he or she has. In this way we begin to pay attention to the person who holds the role, rather than to the role that defines a person. So we begin to hear Lila who is also a grand-mother and MacKenzie who is also a student and Devon who is also an employee, all of whom are much, much more than whatever role in which we meet them. When we meet persons in this way, we see them in a new light. We pay more attention to what they identify as pertinent in a given experience in their lives. It accords dignity to others because it allows them to define their own voice and pertinen-cies. This process begins to break down the walls that we may have constructed in making persons others and helps us to see them as multifaceted human beings. And for educators, it may begin simply by attending Marissa's ballgame or Evan's concert or Chin Fei's Chinese New Year's celebration. When youngsters see their teachers attending such events, the message they receive is that their teacher acknowledges the multiple dimensions of their lives. They are more than the role of a student in a classroom.

This leads us to consider the lack of connection persons feel within a given culture because of its devaluation of others. In order for a society that devalues a group of persons based on a common characteristic to overcome this and learn to sustain dignity, any who dominate must come to know the others as multifaceted persons. Hence, there is a critical need to create authentic connections wherein individuals heretofore defined only as the other can become known and demonstrate their individual dignity.

Recall Polakow's argument in chapter 3 regarding the damaging power of labels to deflect a teacher's attention from the meaning the individual child is making. Consider George, for example. Polakow describes his situation. The child of a young, single mother, small for his age, behind in his school abilities, George transferred from a predominantly black school to a predominantly white, low-income school. He was assigned to the lowest reading group, with a teacher who tells George's classroom teacher, "You'll see how terrible these black students are." Although it is a struggle, George does have some success in his regular classroom and seems to have a flair for writing. But any success in his reading class carries the suspicion of cheating. He is punished for not completing his reading assignments and must miss recess. He complains that his assignments are not completed because he cannot read them. This is not because he cannot *read*, but because the ditto sheets he must fill out are illegible. Here is the response of his teacher as reported by Polakow: "Mrs. Crim claims that George entered school too late in the year for her to request a new workbook and adds, 'What difference would it make. He can't do the work and he doesn't care.'" Such attributions are blatant examples of prejudice and discrimination. George's "dual identity as both a poor and a black child in a school structure that is openly racist and filled with prejudicial stereotypes about children in poverty puts George at the mercy of a forbidding and accusatory adult world."[3]

Would that this were an isolated case, but it is not. Polakow's book tells many like stories. Sometimes the marginalization is not as blatant, but it remains in too many places and is an obstacle that many children face as they enter our schools. When this occurs, as figures of power and authority, teachers interact with these children only as others. While the children truly may have been different than the teachers in a number of respects, the teachers never sought out the meaning that the children placed upon their differences, be they race, ethnicity, ability, or language. The teachers imposed a meaning on the children based upon some rather abstract and general notion of difference, whether it was poverty, single-parentedness, ethnicity, attention deficit disorder, or the myriad of other labels we have to deal with children. What dignity requires is that the teacher pay attention to the meaning the child himself or herself places on his or her own experience, including whatever characteristic creates difference.

In *Lost in Translation,* Eva Hoffman makes an argument for the power of core stories to expand our knowledge and teach us things we did not know. She explains how stories are expansive in this way when she speaks of how she is enlightened as she encounters other stories. "I've grasped a new piece of experience," she says. "It is mine."[4] Stories give a glimpse of experience we might not have had otherwise. Stories are conveyed with emotion that speaks to our minds and hearts. Paley indicates that "once we push deeply into the collective imagination, it is easier to establish connections and build mythologies. . . . The fantasies of any group form the basis of its culture; this is where we search for common ground."[5] Generally, what we know comes from our own experience. In order to reach beyond our own experience, sharing stories allows us to see things as they could be and, in so doing, permits us to search for the common ground of our experience. When education is primarily assumed to be learning a list of facts or a set of skills defined by an externally created curriculum, then there is little room in the school day for the children to bring themselves and their stories to the learning community.

The advantage of stories is that they provide these experiences of coming to know the other in a less threatening way than almost any other form of communication. When a story is told, it does not demand that the hearers change or even accept the account as their own. It only requires that they hear (no simple task, of course). Yet through this process something *does* happen and we do change by virtue of having heard and paid attention to another's story. In this sense, listening to stories and creating connections implies a Gadamerian hermeneutic circle at work. The hermeneutic circle implies that each of us comes to any human activity with a set of preunderstandings which will influence the communication that occurs there. While individuals bring their own pre-understandings to the task, they also hear the understandings of the other. Though this may be difficult, in this passage, Gadamer explains how the hermeneutic circle impacts the meaning we make:

> Of course this does not mean that when we listen to someone or read a book we must forget all our foremeanings concerning the content and all our own ideas. All that is asked is that we remain open to the meanings of the other person or text. But this openness always includes our situating the other meaning in relation to the whole of our own meanings.[6]

By situating the other's meaning in "relation to the whole of our own" we forge a connection or realize a connection that we already share. We cannot connect otherwise because each of us brings with us our foremeanings. It is not that listening to another's story requires that we accept the meanings conveyed in that story, but the connection is created when we "remain open to the meanings of the other person" as Gadamer described.

Remaining open to the meanings of the other may seem easier if we share some of the same frames of reference or foremeanings. While this may be true, it is not an indictment of our ability to connect with others across difference. In *Telling Tales: Making Sense of Christian and Judaic Nonsense,* Jacob Neusner provides another account of how stories create connections between persons with diverse traditions.[7] Neusner argues that contrary to current scholarly understanding, Jews and Christians have never really "heard" each other. While they have held conversations with one another, in actuality they simply talk past one another in their respective traditions. Neusner posits a role for story in mediating the gap that has remained intact between these traditions. This is the role that story can play between any persons who are attempting to make sense of their worlds. The difference between their worlds can be bridged by story in the following way. We know our own tradition. Because of the dialogical and narrative nature of the self, we are an embodiment of our cultural tradition. We can make sense of another's story only as we hear what it resonates with in our own story.[8]

In this regard, what Neusner found problematic in creating authentic dialogue was the inability to make sense of the other within one's own terms, while still retaining something that the other can recognize. Neusner argues that story can provide the form to do that by "listening to the other's story and finding among my stories a tale that tells me what the other feels in the other's story."[9] By way of illustrating his point, Neusner employs a biblical example and asks, "Out of the resources of Judaism how am I to make sense of something so absurd as the notion that God has a mother?" To do this, he calls upon the Judaic story of Rachel wherein the "flight to Egypt in the story of Jesus is represented as a counterpart to the exile of Israel in the time of Jeremiah. Jesus stands for Jeremiah, Mary for Rachel." This example demonstrates that through the story of one culture, "in a direct and parallel way, I can feel some of the feelings that this story in Matthew elicits: the sadness of the mother's love, the providential protection of the mother." The poignant experiences of a mother's loss are common, albeit contextually different. Since story calls upon the experience of the human *emotion* rather than the *event* per se, the psychology and the emotion of the story may be tapped through sharing stories.

I must add that it is not only the emotion of the story that is tapped, but the power of story is that it generates a contextualized type of learning that is not represented in traditional modes of knowledge making. Sara Ruddick speaks to this distinction. She describes having a "love affair with Reason" as she grew up in the world of education. Although she loved and found refuge in them, the standards of rationality and philosophic reason were narrow and limiting. As she continued with life experience, particularly that of falling in love, of becoming a mother, she found herself pushing the edges of Reason, traditionally defined. Through her immediate and contextual experience of mothering, she brought a new dimension to what "counts" as knowledge. Speaking of her daily life that was shared with children and other mothers, she asked, "Could this 'chattering' so unlike the philosophy in which I was trained, be 'thinking?' Did I, did we, through endless telephone calls and late night coffees, create themes of a 'discourse?' "[10] This discourse was a storied discourse and was the means through which knowledge and understanding were generated and shared.

From my preceding discussion I do not mean to imply that there is an easy solution to bridging our differences simply by sharing our stories. I am arguing, along with Ruddick and Neusner, that there is a way to bridge the gap, sometimes chasm, of difference through use of story and an expanded explanation of how it is we know. It is possible although challenging to use story to bridge difference.

There is another type of connectedness that also occurs within the personal realm of dignity. When events occur in lives that cannot easily be explained through the everyday constructs of meaning that an individual has heretofore employed, then story has the ability to accommodate such disruptions. When a temporary gap in meaning occurs (as an inexplicable event or as a denial of experience), rather than deny that the experience has happened, stories have the capacity to knit the new experience into the meaning of the past. The new meaning may fit comfortably with the old, or it may radically change the meaning of the story to date. Or it may be the case that the self will hold this event in abeyance . . . waiting for another time to integrate it into a more coherent system of meaning. When this occurs, Brody indicates that "storytelling heals by restoring a disrupted connectedness."[11] When one is in an introspective mood and trying to make sense of one's experience, storytelling that takes the thickness of contextuality into account can mend the disruptions by making new connections between heretofore disparate experiences.

I recall that in my preparation as a school counselor, I was cautioned not to replace or challenge the meaning of a child who is in an abusive family situation until that child has a coherent and safe way to accommodate a new meaning into his or her life. For example, a child who grows up in a family with a parent who is an alcoholic probably has, among other things, a disrupted sense of meaning and/or some meanings that prevent the flourishing of his or her life. Often, the child places blame on him or herself. He or she might say, "If only I were better . . . then my mom wouldn't drink," or in many instances, a younger child has simply accepted the alcoholism and its consequences as a normal part of life. Yet in counseling (or often later in life), the child's pain attests to the fact that there was a concurrent meaning being created that was simply too painful to accommodate at the time. It would have to wait until later. Story, with its renegotiating of meaning, allows for the grafting in of experiences and events creating a coherent story for the teller. Until this occurs, stories do not disappear. On the contrary, bits and pieces of stories coexist with the larger, more coherent sense of one's life.

The preceding discussion illuminated various descriptions of how core stories sustain dignity by creating connections between persons. These include the noninstrumental use of core stories, the role for authentic voice, the ability for core stories to reveal one's own meaning, the method by which core stories assist us to expand our knowledge and understanding, and the capacity for core stories to accommodate disruptions in meaning.

The second point that I want to make is that stories sustain dignity through their ability to name that which dominates and marginalizes, as well as that which sustains and nurtures dignity. In a public realm, persons can name their concerns and oppressions. In order to overcome that which dominates by avoiding, ignoring, or abusing our dignity, we must be able to name the particular domination. Stories are vehicles for this. Brody indicates that illness occurs when a person is able to "give a name to the complaint—if it has a name, it must have an existence apart from me; so then I can struggle against it."[12] So it is with us when external forces oppress us. When we can give those experiences of oppression a name, the oppression becomes something "out there," separate from us. We do not have to internalize the image given to us by the oppressor. Our dignity is sustained not because we have thrown off all of the oppression, but because we have the ability to "author" our own story.

Whereas actions that dominate and destroy dignity create spaces of silence where no authentic dialogue occurs, creating discursive space for dialogue by naming dominations takes a big step toward sustaining dignity. Such a discursive space provides the heretofore excluded person with what Scott calls an "imaginative breathing space in which the normal categories of order and hierarchy are less than completely inevitable."[13] When, in the sphere of human relations, inevitability, or what appears to be inevitable, is challenged, dialogue can occur.

In like manner, dignity can be sustained when we can name that which is *nurturing* of our dignity. In a culture such as ours, with its glorification of criticism and negativity in the public realm, naming that which is positive may seem odd or old-fashioned. Certainly, naming the positive often is dismissed as that which is trivialized or sentimentalized. But there are ways that we can name that which nourishes our dignity without falling prey to these criticisms. In this regard, bell hooks discusses ways in which we can tie theory to social practice in order to make theory a liberatory practice in the academic realm. Liberatory practice would be a positive contribution, a contribution that nurtured one's dignity. It is theory that begins with the act of naming born out of our own experience. Sometimes that experience has been painful; other times, it has been joyous, but simply invisible to others. Speaking of theory as liberatory practice, hooks reminds us that "our search leads us back to where it all began, to that moment when an individual woman or child, who may have thought she was all alone, . . . began to name her practice, indeed began to formulate theory from lived experience."[14] It is in naming these lived experiences through narrative, through story, that dignity can be sustained.

But what about education? For a moment let us set aside the blatant discrimination apparent in Polakow's descriptions and ask how dignity can be nurtured in the lives of students facing the more subtle forms of psycho-social marginalization. Paulo Freire notes how education can be formulated to nurture and sustain dignity, and in so doing, provide the environment for the flourishing of lives. In order to do this he indicates that the rigid distinction between student and teacher must be dissolved: "The teacher is no longer merely the-one-who-teaches, but one who is himself taught in dialogue with the students, who in turn while being taught also teach. *They become jointly responsible for a process in which all grow*" (emphasis mine).[15] Freire recognizes the narrative nature of human relationships and emphasizes the joint responsibility for gaining understanding. When education is perceived in this light, then other voices that create the public transcript are invited into the dialogue and as they are heard, dignity is affirmed. Stories are being told. According to Freire, it would be the stories of both teacher and students. Bell hooks echoes this requirement. She contends that "when education is the practice of freedom, students are not the only ones who are asked to share, to confess. Engaged pedagogy does not seek simply to empower students. Any classroom that employs a holistic model of learning will also be a place where teachers grow."[16]

In summary, core stories have the power to sustain human dignity in two significant ways that impact both the personal and the social/relational realms of dignity. The first is by their ability to create or reveal connections between persons. These means of making connections are diverse and include nourishing the equality of regard that morally should be given to one another's stories, acknowledging the position of the self as primary author of that story. Additionally, stories make it harder for us simply to regard persons as others or as objects for our means. This is accomplished in part as one reveals the meaning of experience for himself or herself, allowing us to come to know others in a way that goes beyond superficial definitions constitutive of role constructions. Stories enable us to see the particular understandings, values, and concerns of another's life. Stories have the potential to transcend cultural difference by connecting with the commonalities of emotional response, and in a very personal way, story can encompass breaks in meaning, and as one mends such breaks throughout a life, coherence is maximized and one connects with oneself.

The second way that stories sustain dignity is by opening the public dialogue or conversation by allowing the naming of that which either marginalizes or nurtures dignity. As individuals add unique voices to the public conversation, they become party to culturally negotiated meaning. Story assists in creating a particular type of public. School is one of the spaces for the sharing of stories to occur. In addition, core stories are vehicles for naming oppressions and dominations that wear away at dignity. Such oppressions and dominations must be exhumed before full dignity can flourish.

TELLERS AND LISTENERS

Because storytelling has such powerful potential to sustain and enhance dignity, it is morally important to identify the responsibilities that accompany such an endeavor. As in all things that have the potential to affect deeply human lives, one must be aware of the potential for harm. In this sense, my claim is that dignity requires that we not abuse stories, but honor them. Hence it becomes important to make a distinction between the two parties involved in the activity of telling stories and what their responsibilities may be. The two parties involved in the endeavor of storytelling are the one who tells a story and the one who hears the story.[17] While an individual possesses a story regardless of whether another one receives it, it is in *receiving* another's story that one can enhance the other's dignity. Said another way, it is in feeling one's story *received* that one's dignity is sustained. Making a claim to dignity is an individual act, while sustaining or ascribing dignity is a social act as listeners respond. Hence, dignity requires a breadth of social relations to flourish.

What are the responsibilities for each, teller and listener, in this process of storytelling? While the responsibility to hear rests with the listener, the teller also has some special obligations. Hoffman poignantly tells us of her struggle to pay attention to stories throughout the changes in her life. She reminds us that we are the "keepers of each other's stories, and the shape of these stories has unfolded in part from our interwoven accounts." She then goes on to suggest our obligation as storytellers by describing the work between herself and a friend:

> Human beings don't only search for meanings, they are themselves units of meaning; but we can mean something only within the fabric of larger significations. Miriam is one of the people through whom I've gained a meaning here. Starting so far apart, we have, through painstaking back and forth, forged a language in common. We keep describing the flow of experience to each other with the impetus of truth, and thus we keep creating new maps and tapestries of a shared reality.[18]

A teller's responsibility is to be involved in forging a meaning while accepting the risks of being as truthful and authentic as is possible. In storytelling, both tellers and listeners have an obligation to be as authentic as possible. When Taylor speaks of authenticity as being

the background for the development of the self, he also posits that
the self is dialogical in nature. As I described in chapter 4, the self
defines its identity "always in dialogue with, sometimes in struggle
against, the identities our significant others want to recognize in
us."[19] This dialogical development of selves also requires that we be
open to what Taylor calls "horizons of significance." These horizons
represent the "background of things that matter." Taylor describes
what role these background horizons play:

> But to bracket out history, nature, society, the demands of soli-
> darity, everything but what I find in myself, would be to elimi-
> nate all candidates for what matters. Only if I exist in a world in
> which history, or the demands of nature, or the needs of my
> fellow human beings, or the duties of citizenship, or the call of
> God, or something else of this order matters crucially, can I
> define an identity for myself that is not trivial. Authenticity is not
> the enemy of demands that emanate from beyond the self; it
> supposes such demands.[20]

In order for persons to be authentic, they must recognize the
nature of horizons of significance, their own and others', and be
open to them. These horizons of significance often are conveyed
through narrative storytelling, representing that which each person
defines as significant. Horizons of significance represent those things
that create the larger tapestry of our life situated within a culture.
They may include religion, history, human nature, and relationships.
In an effort to be authentic, tellers must attempt to represent their
own horizons, as well as learn about and listen to the horizons of
others. Listeners must listen with an "ear" that acknowledges hearing
against one's own horizons.

As noted earlier, the notion of telling a story implies a listener.
As can be seen above, the process of gaining authenticity, understanding, and dignity is an interactive process. It is not simply one
person speaking and another listening, but it entails an ongoing
process of creating oneself as one understands another. It works like
this. As I come to know another more closely, my own understanding
of myself and my horizons of significance are enhanced. So the
burden that accrues to the hearer in this dialogical process begins
with having, as Brody says, a "profound respect for the power of
individuals to shape their own stories."[21] This is an acknowledgment
of the dignity of persons as moral agents. From this point, listeners

must be aware of their responsibility to create environments where the sharing of core stories can occur. It is not to force storytelling, for that would be domination. When a story is told, the hearer must listen, must "attend carefully to the stories . . . and engage . . . in meaningful conversation, within the broader context of the range of life stories made available to all of us by our society and our culture."[22] Again, this points to the need for teachers to open up spaces in the school day for story "telling" to emerge.

Another important responsibility for the listener focuses on motivation. One can be interested in stories for a variety of reasons that range from benign to malicious intents. For example, one could be interested in stories for purposes of manipulating others or because there was a purpose one wished to impose on another. But these instrumental reasons are not the ones that respect human dignity. In order for stories to enhance and sustain dignity, there must be a commitment to listen to another's story for the sake of coming to know the other, for nurturing or sustaining his or her dignity or right to create a unique life, rather than to dominate or use the other's story to advance or serve one's own purpose. We are all familiar with the classic family example when a parent lives his or her own dreams through a child's activities. When the child is participating in an activity for the benefit of the parent, the child becomes swallowed up by the parent's story. The once intrinsic enjoyment of the activity lessens, and the child often "burns out," rather than growing in skills, competency, and understanding.

THE DOMINATION OF STORIES

It is important to understand how dignity and hence core stories are insulted or diminished so that we may avoid domination ourselves. It is important to talk about the ways that stories are limited, dominated, and extinguished since that is the essence of psychosocial marginalization. Some of this discussion will sound similar to the earlier discussion in chapter 3 about the ways psycho-social marginalization occurs. At the risk of redundancy, it is crucial to hone in specifically on how stories are dominated. In fact, if my argument is sound, there should be redundancy here because I have argued that dignity is sustained only as persons are respected in their ability to create their lives. Creating one's life entails identity and meaning making, which is carried through story. Hence, the marginalization of the self should appear similar to the domination of stories.

As human beings, when we meet the other morally, generally there is as great a potential for harm as there is for good. Tragically, we have seen this within the dynamics of the family. On the one hand, families may be wonderful seedbeds for developing human potential and loving, unique individuals; on the other hand, families may do irreparable harm to developing persons. So it is with the use of stories. The notion of story also can be misused, yet this should not stop the discussion of the power of stories to sustain dignity and overcome marginalization. In this section I will speak to the ways stories may be misused and dominated.

Brody indicates that there are two ways to demolish life narratives or core stories. This can occur when one leaves out a portion of a narrative or it can occur when one reverses the narrative or interferes with the links that the teller finds pertinent. Describing what happens to persons' stories when this occurs, Brody says, "These assaults effectively render the narrative meaningless and destroy the power of the narrative itself to offer meaning to other events."[23] What these two forms of interference have in common is that they are attempts by a listener to dominate the story and decide what is pertinent. They ignore the importance of the relationship between authorship and dignity. This form of domination can be seen most easily in many instances of emotional abuse where the one who dominates forces the account of what occurred onto the abused, even to the point of defining the feelings and motivations that the abused may have. The more intensely this occurs, the more human dignity is shattered because it denies the acknowledgment of the equal human standing of another and his or her responsibility to be an autonomous author of her or his own story.

This kind of domination is not reserved for abusive situations. Given the human condition, there are always times when our needs are not being met in one way or another as we bump into someone else's project. It is at the intersection where two core stories meet that we must be careful that we do not usurp the meaning of another. Imagine a parent or a teacher trying to calm a child after an angry outburst. "Oh, you didn't really mean that! You were just angry." Where is the space for the child to "own" what he or she did mean? Or perhaps a child is interested in pursuing a career in the arts, when his parents have envisioned a high school preparation and college career in the sciences in order to be financially successful. In many little ways, we confront the dilemma of intersecting stories every day.

Domination undermines story's role in preserving dignity. It occurs throughout much of our lives. Although many of the ways domination occurs are subtle, they are powerful in their ability to make persons and their contexts invisible. Richard Wright provides a poignant glimpse into the depth of harm that accrued to him when his story was not heard and his dignity not held in esteem. Recall that he writes of domination and its power to make one invisible, even to oneself:

> Not only had the southern whites not known me, but, more important still, as I had lived in the South I had not had the chance to learn who I was. The pressure of southern living kept me from being the kind of person that I might have been. I had been what my surroundings had demanded, what my family— conforming to the dictates of the whites above them—had exacted of me, and what the whites had said that I must be. Never being fully able to be myself, I had slowly learned that the South could recognize but a part of a man, could accept but a fragment of his personality, and all the rest—the best and deepest things of heart and mind—were tossed away in blind ignorance and hate.[24]

What Wright identifies as so devastating about the marginalization that he experienced was that he was unable even to come to know himself because of the near total domination of his story. He was marginalized stereotypically by the domination of the whites. He also faced psycho-social marginalization because his family also conformed to the "dictates of the whites above them." There was no room for a hidden transcript to moderate the impacts of the racism in his life. There was no room for him to author his own life. That would have been the demand of dignity, that is, that the social context around him provide the room for his life story to flourish. That did not happen. In this horrible loss, the "best and deepest things of heart and mind" were never acknowledged.

Forms of invisibility are all around us. Perhaps in schools children are disciplined for misbehavior without their teachers' understanding that they may be hungry because there is no food at home. Or perhaps children are measured, categorized, and rewarded for scores they achieve on tests rather than celebrated for the achievement in their stories. These examples and others like them point to the inability of storytellers to have a voice in what occurs in their daily lives. They are made invisible and are seen only as instrumental ends to someone else's goals. Yet dignity requires us to pay attention to and respect the creation of the life of the self. Paley makes the distinction that paying attention to a person's stories does not require conformity or equal treatment. Rather what is being argued for is the "equal *opportunity* to demand special treatment" (emphasis mine).[25] This is a demand for authorship. Dignity requires that persons have the opportunity to create their lives. One creates a life by articulating meaning, and meaning is carried through narrative. Without providing those opportunities in our schools, we must ask ourselves as well, What are the "best and deepest things of heart and mind" that we may be missing in the students who pass through our classes?

Stories are likewise extinguished when the story of one who dominates comes to eclipse the story of persons who have an established story. For example, in *When Jesus Came, the Corn Mothers Went Away*, Ramon Gutierrez documents what occurred in the culture of the native people when the Europeans arrived in North America and brought with them not only their dominating story, but their belief in instrumental ends.[26] Not only was there a collision of ideology, but there was a collision of valued paradigms for how one understands the world. While it was obvious that ideologies such as myths of creation were different between these two groups, the Europeans propagated the idea that the very notion of "myth" was not good enough as an explanatory construct and had to be replaced with a scientific explanation. While the model of scientific explanation is crucial to a modern society, it is important to get clear about the nature of the knowledge we choose to embrace. In this case, the story of the dominator nearly obliterated the story of the native peoples who had tended this continent. And as our current history evidences, our various indigenous peoples have almost been obliterated by the domination of their stories. Such is the link between story and selfhood.

Another way story can be vulnerable to domination is by providing only prepackaged experiences for students. Rather than having students explore and generate their own inquiry, a piece of the curriculum puzzle is neatly handed to them. Such prepackaging may actually prevent the formation of individual stories, that is, prevent students from creating and revising meaning by placing new knowledge and understanding into their existent system of meaning. The study of history provides fertile ground for illustration. For generations, students in public schools have learned of the "discovery of America" by Christopher Columbus. Many of us celebrated it by cutting out construction paper sailing ships and by memorizing rhymes. It was not until recent years that this packaged interpretation was questioned by those who represented heretofore silenced voices. By presenting this interpretation of a historical event as unproblematic, there was no room for students to develop their own meanings about it. In contrast, now that there are interpretations that challenge the traditional story, students can be given room to place this event within their own system of meaning. Prepackaging of education can be contrasted with Paulo Freire's model of learning that rejects the "banking" notion of education, in which students are simply empty vessels waiting to be filled with discrete fragments of knowledge.[27]

But the prepackaging of curriculum is not only a problem in history classes to be solved by adopting a multicultural focus. Giving up the paradigm that represents a "banking" education model means that fundamentally we must change our mindset or gestalt about what it means to educate. Simply employing new educational practice without a fundamental shift in how one views education will fall short. For example, I still see nods of affirmation from contemporary students when I describe being in my eighth-grade science class. Science was my favorite subject, and I was very excited to be in a science classroom where we would really perform experiments. (Nowadays they would be called "hands-on" activities.) The room had raised lab stations instead of desks, stools instead of chairs; we had Bunsen burners and beakers and safety goggles. But an interesting thing happened that year. Instead of my love of science growing, it waned as it became clear that we were not truly engaging in scientific experimentation. Rather, we were under pressure to replicate prepackaged lab experiments and results. If the findings in our lab reports were not correct, then we received a poor grade. Recall Dewey's educational caveat: *Seeming* to be scientists replaced *being* scientists. The result, for the student is a gradual disengagement from the curriculum and activities of schooling. The prepackaging of curriculum did not allow me to bring my sense of meaning making to the educational task.

A listener's superficiality also can dominate stories. In educational settings, this may occur in the form of multicultural truisms.

What is originally meant as a thorough attempt to educate people about the diversity of persons and how cultural differences create different relational expectations and values, truisms about a particular culture are distilled into superficial statements which continue stereotyping and perpetuate marginalization. This occurs as teachers who are trying to heed these truisms miss seeing and hearing the child and the meaning that child is giving to his or her life. For example, a cultural truism might be, "Don't demand eye contact from such and such a cultural group when you speak to them." When this approach is used superficially, educators are relating to only a representation of a cultural group and not to an individual and, once again, miss the individual meaning.

Supplementing our understanding of the notion of superficiality, Megan Boler speaks to the damage wrought by decontextualizing the story. She indicates that when we present the story of another people without including its complex and multifaceted context, we do students a disservice by having them think they have captured the experience of a particular people. For example, students might read Anne Frank's *Diary* or Art Spiegelman's *Maus* about the Holocaust experience. Having read one book or story about the group's experience, students may mistakenly walk away saying, "Ahh . . . now I know what it was like to be Jewish during this difficult time." Developing empathy is a worthy goal of sharing stories, but when it is done superficially, it dominates rather than nurtures because it stops students from pressing on for deeper understanding. Rather, Boler argues that storytelling also must entail an obligation on the part of the hearer.[28] This obligation would be borne of understanding the contextuality of the story. In the example provided, if the stories were couched within a multiperspective historical context, students would come away with a better understanding of what their obligation would be to ensure that such a horrific event did not occur again. They could not walk away with the story of another neatly tied up in a package? Instead, such stories would, of necessity, impinge upon them.

In summary, stories can be dominated in a variety of ways. Teachers who are committed to using stories in their classrooms need to be aware not only of how stories sustain dignity, but of how stories may be misused to dominate. Using stories to replace others' stories (thereby creating invisibility), neglecting contextuality, prepackaging, and fragmenting are all ways that stories may be dominated and used to marginalize. They ignore or "freeze" children's lives, rather than assisting them to engage in identity development and meaning-making activities.

Paying attention to a contextually storied life gives us the opportunity to come to know the world of the other. Not paying attention to individual lives and sustaining the dignity of others bears a cost we should not be willing to pay. The cost speaks to the moral commitment we have to the dignity of all persons and the concurrent development of their lives. Bruner aptly describes the social cost that accrues when the narrative resources that allow stories to be generated and told are slim. He states:

> There is breakdown that results from sheer impoverishment of narrative resources—in the permanent underclass or the urban ghetto, in the second and third generation of the Palestinian refugee compound, in the hunger-preoccupied villages of semipermanently drought-stricken villages in sub-Saharan Africa. It is not that there is a total loss in putting story form to experience, but that the "worst scenario" story comes so to dominate daily life that variation seems no longer to be possible.[29]

While this cost speaks to the societal implications, the underlying cost is to human dignity and the diminished capacity for an individual to generate and tell a story. It is not simply an urban ghetto or an anonymous refugee camp we must confront. It is the loss of a rich narrative landscape upon which young people can draw to create their own stories. If it is true that a worst case scenario could dominate one's life, then how could children ever imagine that things could be otherwise? What role does story play in this imagining?

It is to these questions that we now turn. My concluding chapter argues that conceiving education as paying attention to stories can create the conditions necessary for the dignity of children to be sustained and hence for their lives to flourish.

7

Paying Attention to Stories:
Education and Dignity

Education and Dignity

I will begin this concluding chapter by reviewing the argument I have set forth in order to situate a discussion of education and dignity. Recall that I argued that in order to sustain or nurture someone's dignity, we must recognize one another's right to create one's own life. Further, I stated that creating a life includes the tasks of identity development and meaning making. Due to the narrative construction of the self, identity and meaning are developed and expressed through storied form. Therefore, sustaining or nurturing dignity would entail paying attention to stories.

Now, turning our attention to the relationship between education and stories: when education is conceived as growth and development as Dewey envisioned, and when a concern for the growth and development of their students is implied in the responsibility of teaching, then the adults involved in education must pay special attention to the growth and development of the children in their care. Because growth and development implicate identity formation and meaning making, and because identity formation and meaning making are supported by paying attention to stories, adults who

113

educate in schools must pay attention to the stories of the children in their midst. Because education requires a proactive stance towards the development of children, it is the case that adults not only should care about not harming children, but also should be engaged in activities that assist children's lives to flourish. Hence, if schools are to pay attention to the dignity of children's lives, they must pay attention to the stories children are making, that is, the sense and meaning they are trying to make of their lives. To do otherwise would be to miseducate.

If we take seriously the notion that in all our educational endeavors we must be committed to preserving dignity, then it will be important to create spaces for stories to be heard. Calling upon the notion of core story creates a richer understanding of what it means to pay attention to individual lives and the meaning that each life is continually creating anew. The power of stories rests in the way that core stories allow us to pay attention to individual lives within a relational context. That in turn sustains the dignity of those lives.

As we talk of school renewal, we need to ask ourselves how our conversations would be different if our fundamental goal were to sustain and enhance dignity and create spaces for children to flourish. Certainly, we would continue to talk of instructional strategies and curricula, citizenship, vocational training, and other tasks of schooling. But if the fundamental commitment in education were to sustaining dignity, then our conversations and subsequent solutions might look different indeed. This chapter will speak to what such an education might entail. Utilizing the notion of core story means that we pay attention to individual lives and that the relationships we have are characterized by a deep notion of care and respect. I have argued that stories are a powerful way for us to pay attention to lives because they are necessary to sustain a moral commitment to dignity.

Let us look at an example from which we might draw some observations about the role of dignity in the schools. I draw upon the personal narrative of bell hooks, who describes what school was like in the rural South before forced desegregation. She writes:

> Almost all our teachers at Booker T. Washington were black women. They were committed to nurturing intellect so that we could become scholars, thinkers, and cultural workers—black folks who used our "minds." We learned early that our devotion to learning, to a life of the mind, was a counter-hegemonic act, a fundamental way to resist every strategy of white racist coloni-

zation. Though they did not define or articulate these practices in theoretical terms, my teachers were enacting a revolutionary pedagogy of resistance that was profoundly anticolonial. Within these segregated schools, black children who were deemed exceptional, gifted, were given special care. Teachers worked with and for us to ensure that we would fulfill our intellectual destiny and by so doing uplift the race. My teachers were on a mission. To fulfill that mission, my teachers made sure they "knew" us. They knew our parents, our economic status, where we worshipped, what our homes were like, and how we were treated in the family. . . . Attending school then was sheer joy.[1]

In this passage one gleans a sense of the dignity that hooks was afforded by her teachers at Booker T. Washington, dignity even in the midst of a historical period where horrible overt racism was the order of the day, racism that actually created the environment where this particular segregated school was located. What was occurring in this school in order that children's lives might flourish and their dignity be sustained and nurtured? How can we name the characteristics of this educative experience? To begin, teachers in this school had a sense of mission and dedication to the child, but also to a larger social good. The education they provided did not perpetuate the status quo, but challenged it. In this school, teachers "knew" the child in a rich sense. They knew the context within which each child lived; they envisioned the potential of each child, understanding that each child brought distinct gifts with him or her. They understood the story of each child, a story that sometimes stretched across generations. These teachers were incredibly optimistic, though they must have known the deep despair of racism.

Unfortunately, these characteristics cannot be extrapolated from this wonderful school and then placed like a template on every school in America. It was the whole of the context that created a powerful school that sustained the dignity of its children. It was the character of the moral relationships that occurred there that allowed lives to flourish.[2] Hooks' proclamation that "attending school . . . was sheer joy" attests to the fact that her dignity was intact and the attention being paid to her life allowed it to flourish. Of the children I know today, even among those who enjoy school, I cannot imagine any of them suggesting that attending school is "sheer joy." Sometimes school may be fun or enjoyable, but joy connotes a deeper sense of significance that accompanied the education hooks received.

If it is generally the case that children do not find joy in their education, then we would want to know what the characteristics of an education are that sustain and nurture the dignity of a child and that lead to a sense of joy in learning.

To help answer that, we can look at the character of education that hooks subsequently faced in the desegregated school she was forced to attend. Identifying the differences between the two types of education hooks received may shed light on what characteristics are important to an education that pays attention to the life of a child. Describing her desegregated school, hooks explains:

> School changed utterly with racial integration. Gone was the messianic zeal to transform our minds and beings that had characterized teachers and their pedagogical practices in our all-black schools. Knowledge was suddenly about information only. It had no relation to how one lived, behaved. . . . When we entered racist, desegregated, white schools we left a world where teachers believed that to educate black children rightly would require a political commitment. Now, we were mainly taught by white teachers whose lessons reinforced racist stereotypes. For black children, education was no longer about the practice of freedom. Realizing this, I lost my love of school. . . . That shift from beloved, all-black schools to white schools where black students were always seen as interlopers, as not really belonging, taught me the difference between education as the practice of freedom and education that merely strives to reinforce domination.[3]

What do we learn from this? While this second type of education has deep implications regarding stereotypical marginalization, it also has telling implications for teachers who are concerned with the subtle and pervasive psycho-social marginalization. In this school, education was not about the "practice of freedom" or the flourishing of children's lives. Rather, we sense the domination of lives by the forced anonymity, by the lack of respect, by envisioning education merely as information passing. Lost was the sense of community or a relational world. Such a relational world is a necessary ingredient in education that pays attention to stories.

Hooks is not implying that we should return to the pre–civil rights era when African Americans were legally separated from Euro Americans in schools and other public places. Rather, she juxtaposes these two experiences of schooling to highlight the significance of

their differences. In addition, this contrast brings into focus the attributes of a learning community and a community of solidarity. She
asks the reader to consider the unforeseen consequences of what was
lost when that community was fractured. From these two very different educative experiences described by hooks, we may conclude that
an education that envisions itself as sustaining and nurturing the dignity of children would pay attention to the following.

Teachers would make efforts to know each child as a unique
individual. They would strive to know about his or her life, family,
and interests. Paying attention to who the child is implies a relationship between teacher and student. A relationship where persons are
known to each other counteracts anonymity and invisibility. Counteracting anonymity can be undertaken in various ways. For Deborah
Meier at Central Park East Schools, it was through creating a small
school where people literally could pay attention to one another's
lives. For Carole Williams at B. F. Day Elementary, it was asking her
teachers to visit the shelters where their homeless students lived. The
impact was profound. For others, it is in attending a student's ball
game, inviting one of your students who is in band to play some
blues during your unit on African American history, to have a parent
or grandparent come to your class and tell the students a story about
growing up. It could be that you live, work, and play in the community where you teach so that you rub shoulders with the parents and
children of your school. There are many ways for us to dispel the
cloak of invisibility.

Teachers would have a sense of mission about their teaching,
manifest in two ways. First, they would care about the child him or
herself, and, second, they would possess a sense of a greater social
good to be sought in their teaching. In hooks' case, education was
about the "practice of freedom." Every teacher and every school
should have a sense of what education should be about, on a broad
societal level, as well as what it means for each child.[4] Since we do
not yet have a flawless society, there is plenty of room to challenge
the status quo in an attempt to develop a society that is more just
and humane. Listen to the words of George S. Counts, who decades
ago worried about the direction in which our society was moving.
His call to teachers was to "assume unprecedented social responsibilities" in order to create a nation "born for better things." He
commented that to "refuse to face the task of creating a vision of a
future America immeasurably more just and noble and beautiful
than the America of today is to evade the most crucial, difficult, and

important educational task."[5] The teachers at Booker T. Washington saw both that their children and our society were "born for better things." This belief animated their teaching and was instilled in their students.

Teachers must provide a sense of optimism in their teaching. We see from hooks' experience that having a sense of optimism does not preclude acknowledging painful circumstances in life. But for education to be empowering, it must engender hope. Kohl reminds us that the "ability to see the world other than it is plays a major role in sustaining hope. It keeps part of one's mind free of the burden of everyday misery and can become a corner of sanity as one struggles to undo the horrors of an unkind and mad world."[6] Certainly, in the days of legally enforced segregation, the world was unkind. Teaching so as to help students imagine and name how the world could be otherwise is a method that sustains hope and optimism.

Teachers must create a sense of belonging so that children do not feel like the interlopers that hooks described. Often, it is stereotypic marginalization that creates interlopers, as children are encountered and dismissed as Hispanic children or project children or attention deficit disorder children. But children also can be made into interlopers by virtue of their own individual characteristics, such as the child who rarely talks, the child who misbehaves, the child who is always in dirty and worn clothing. Beyond making individual children interlopers, I wonder if how we "do" school sometimes makes our own students interlopers. For example, a colleague once posed the following. She queried, "In an elementary school, what area of the building belongs to the children? Where do students have a sense of ownership, responsibility, and place?"

"Of course," we answered, "their classrooms." And we imagined colorfully decorated student rooms with cubbies, clusters of desks, a hamster or two, and student artwork.

"Yes," she replied. "Now think of junior and high schools. What place belongs to the children? Where are they at home?" We thought for a moment, and our puzzled faces gave way to her answer. "The hallways," she said. "In high schools, students own the hallways. The classrooms do not belong to them. They move from period to period, semester to semester. We have left them the hallways, and they have claimed them." This metaphorical analysis is telling when it comes to reflecting on the status of students as interlopers. Rather than leaving our students to the hallways, in what ways might we use our buildings to create spaces where students feel that they belong?

Counteracting invisibility, having a sense of mission, providing hope and optimism, and creating a sense of belonging describe ways that educators can sustain the dignity of the child. Each requires paying some particular attention to the core stories of our students.

SCHOOL AS A PUBLIC PLACE

Recall that I have argued that sustaining and nurturing dignity are not solitary endeavors. Both marginalization and sustaining dignity take place in a social and relational world. Given a desire to decrease those events and relationships that marginalize others, we are left to ask, What kind of a social world or public would best sustain the dignity of lives? Or worded slightly differently, In what type of public could lives flourish? In this section I will draw from three notions of public in order to suggest an understanding of school as a public place where lives can have dignity and flourish.

Thomas Green provides a model of the "public" that both creates and sustains community. While Green is talking more generally about the character of civic life today, I employ his analysis of the public to enrich our understanding of the specific public nature of education. He argues and I agree that we lack a substantive public and that this deficit impinges on the quality of the public education we offer. Green argues that we lack a substantive public because we do not understand the role of public speech that is required to create and sustain one. He states:

> Without public speech there is no public, only a babble of lamentations and complaints, pleadings, pronouncements, claims and counter-claims. Without public speech, the public dies, politics turns to polemics, becomes partisan in the worst sense, even venomous, and we are left with nothing we can reasonably speak of as public education, public service, or public life.[7]

In order to create a public that would mitigate these circumstances, Green provides an analysis of how speech constitutes such a public. He indicates that a public is formed by two types of speech. The first is a type of speech he calls "forum" speech. This is a speech with which we are most acquainted in education. It is the speech of inquiry. This type of speech provides scientific, logical, and philosophical knowledge claims to be used as reasons supporting given propositions. But Green argues that there is another type of speech, often overlooked, that is crucial to forming a vibrant public: it is "umbilical" speech. Umbilical speech is narrative in nature and has its "own objectivity or inter-subjectivity, but not the kind that belongs to truth claims and investigations of science. This is not the speech of inquiry; it is the speech of membership. It is the speech of some public, not because it pronounces public truth, but because it appeals to an umbilical story of some membership."[8] Umbilical speech is storied speech; it is the speech of stories that serve to connect us through the sharing of experience, of tradition, of summoning common ideals. This speech calls upon membership, memory, and connection. Yet it is not a speech that sanctions the status quo that may be exclusionary. It is speech that strives to be inclusive within an ever-widening circle of membership.

Umbilical speech can be inclusive only when it occurs with what Green names the "auditory principle." The auditory principle requires that public speech have an auditor, a listener, and that "public speech occurs when what is said in one person's speech is heard by others as candidates for their own speech."[9] Listening with this qualifier in mind, a shared or public space is carved out as the auditory principle requires that stories be heard. It does not exclude stories; on the contrary, it encourages them. In addition, story or narrative of the "umbilical" type creates a public space as it draws upon or creates shared connections. Judgment by the listener is not immediate. Rather, the listener must "entertain" the story of the other before making judgment or responding. (This is unlike so much of our moral discourse where persons appear to be formulating their typical rebuttals while the speaker is still talking!) Its purpose is not to separate or isolate as "forum" speech or the speech of inquiry and truth-claims sometimes does. Rather, its purpose is to create a community or public where the stories of umbilical speech are valued.

Education as paying attention to stories would incorporate learning how to listen as if the stories of others could be our own. Listening in this way requires imagination.[10] Green cautions us that "declining to listen or to hear another is among our more efficient ways of denying that those others even exist. It is one way of killing them. By rendering such persons inaudible, we make them invisible and, in effect, non-existent."[11] While invisibility marginalizes persons, creating a space for the sharing of "umbilical" stories sustains the dignity of those articulating them. Since individuals use narrative to organize meaning in their lives, narrative functions as a powerful human connector. Polkinghorne indicates that narrative is "not locked within a personal existence: it transcends us as individuals as we communicate our personal thoughts and experiences to others, and as we, in turn, participate as hearers and viewers of their expressions."[12] In this way, narrative transcends individual stories in order to create a public where stories are shared. A public that does not neglect umbilical stories is one where persons are not made invisible, but are connected.[13]

Two other discussions of particular types of social worlds will enrich our understanding of the role of the public in sustaining dignity through paying attention to stories. First, I return to bell hooks, who describes growing up in her rural, southern, black community:

> It was the world of Southern, rural, black growing up, of folks sitting on porches day and night, of folks calling your mama, 'cause you walked by and didn't speak, and of the switch waiting when you got home so you could be taught some manners. It was a world of single older black women schoolteachers, dedicated, tough; they had taught your mama, her sisters, and her friends. They knew your people in ways that you never would and shared their insight, keeping us in touch with generations. It was a world where we had a history.[14]

What can we glean from this passage? The type of community or public that existed here was one where people knew each other and took responsibility for each other. It was an intergenerational community. It had common standards, and it had a history, even though that history seemed somewhat enigmatic to the children who occupied that place and time. It was the children who struggled to integrate the need for civil rights guarantees with a longing for the safety and comfort of their community as they knew it.

In the community hooks knows, she tells of eating a red, ripe tomato from her granddaddy's garden. At that time, she did not know that her granddaddy was a sharecropper, or even understand what that term meant. Rather, she knew he "owned" the land, "it had to be his land, 'cause he worked it, 'cause he held that dirt in his hands and taught you to love it." In her mind, that created ownership, loving it, working it, investing ourselves in it. These also would be characteristics of schools who care about creating such a public space.

What do these characteristics mean for schools and educators who desire to create the type of public that sustains dignity? Such schools would have to generate and sustain meaningful traditions.

Such a school would be intergenerational in character, where persons of many ages work, play, and learn together. A school of this sort would have common standards of excellence, as well as many metaphorical "porches" on which to sit and share umbilical stories.

Let me share a story about responsibility for one another and the role of common standards. These are not insignificant matters. I recall the time a parent shared her acute disappointment in her children's school community. At the end of a school day, as children were rushing out of classrooms and to the busses, this mother was walking through the school grounds to meet her youngest daughter. She was appalled to witness a fourth grader using horribly offensive language at the top of his lungs directed toward another student. What was appalling to this mother was that a teacher walked by this outburst and said nothing to the student. As he noticed the surprise and concern on the face of the mother, he sheepishly smiled and shrugged his shoulders in the direction of the offending child and said, "Glad he's not in my class." The parent's impulse was to march this young person to the office or to read him her own version of the riot act. But taking a cue from this teacher, she also did nothing. So what is the point? The point is that a community cannot be sustained without joint responsibility for the persons there and without agreed upon common standards. Adult educators need to care about children. Yet in this case, it was the teacher's indifference that led to the parent's indifference; and possibly it was the potential for parental retribution that led to the teacher's indifference. No one held this child to the standard of excellence envisioned by this school. Rather than accepting the obligation to create such a community, the blame for breakdown in standards of excellence often is laid at the feet of the children and their homes. But as hooks' example points out, it is the obligation of all in the community to care for the young people.

Sometimes behavior standards can become elevated into the all-important goal, and then domination occurs as children's lives are made secondary to keeping order. Rather than creating an authentic community where a self-disciplined student body is the natural outcome, educators sometimes place the cart before the horse and create a litany of rules designed to create an orderly learning community, only to find that because the rules come before the concern for students, behavior—vandalism, skipping class, and so on—is always a problem. But that is not the image of the community hooks' described. Nor is it the community that a school who cares about the dignity of children would want to create. Young people will push and strain and tug at the boundaries given them, as well they should. But just as important is that those boundaries exist and that there is a multivocal affirmation of those standards. The standards of such a community exist, not in the abstract or for keeping order, but in recognition of the need to provide a healthy and safe place where children can flourish. Christopher Lasch describes how standards assist young people to grow and develop their lives. He states:

> We do children a terrible disservice, however, by showering them with undeserved approval. The kind of reassurance they need comes only with a growing ability to met impersonal standards of competence. Children need to risk failure and disappointment, to overcome obstacles, to face down the terrors that surround them. Self-respect cannot be conferred; it has to be earned. Current therapeutic and pedagogical practice, all "empathy" and "understanding," hopes to manufacture self-respect without risk. Not even witch doctors could perform a medical miracle on that order.[15]

The school that nurtures and sustains dignity is the one that provides the environment for these risks and the space for "facing down the terrors" that come while growing.

Finally, I draw again upon the work of Christopher Lasch who provides another example of a public or community that will assist lives to flourish. He borrows the term *third places* from Oldenburg and describes them as places that are somewhere between the structured formal world of work and bureaucracy and that of the intimate world of the family. The public, as Lasch describes it, requires having this third place. The third place is a "meeting ground midway between the workplace and the family circle, between the "rat race" and the "womb." Third places are situated near where we live. They may be the coffee houses or pubs or synagogues or community center. Lasch indicates that these places are distinct because they are spaces where conversation can flourish, where "people can talk without constraint, except for the constraints imposed by the art of conversation itself." They are places for the telling of umbilical stories, not for the process of inquiry. What is valued in third places is decency. Lasch tells us that "decency is more highly regarded in the third place than wealth or brilliant achievement."[16] He indicates that one's neighbors are more interested in how you live (live with them and others in community) than how well your business does or how brilliant your research may be. Decency is the stuff that binds a community.

What characteristics can we gather from Lasch's description of third places and apply to schools who strive to pay attention to children's lives? I return to the sense of place. Third places are found where people live. Schools also should be situated where people live in order not to force a separation between the community and the school. Public schools that are situated where people live take the first step in being inclusive, that is, they take who is there rather than sorting through applications and selecting students on the basis of preformed criteria. This inclusivity resonates with honoring the creation of one's life. Exclusivity says, in effect, "You can create your life here only if it matches what we are doing." External pressure of this sort compromises the ability to create one's own life in an authentic way as described in chapter 4.

A school that is like a third place would be concerned with having conversation flourish. For conversation or dialogue to flourish, there would be a sense of informality that allows for exploring places heretofore unimagined. For conversation to flourish, there cannot be a rigid and limited agenda. Such limits would stunt conversation, conveying the message that one can only go so far or only broach certain topics. For conversation to flourish, there has to be time and place to be with one another away from carefully determined tasks.

Last, the characteristic we can glean from the third places is that a concern for how one lives, or decency, may be more important than the achievement one attains. It seems to me that such a prioritizing is correct. This is not to say that achievement is unimportant, but it is to make the moral claim that decency or how one treats the other must be prior to the achievement one attains and not vice versa. If achievement is not mediated, then lives may be hurt. In this way, the third place bestows a particular character on the public that is concerned with the flourishing of lives.

In summary, envisioning school as a particular type of public provides a variety of necessary, but not sufficient, conditions for education to occur that will sustain and nurture the dignity of children. I use the term *variety* here because each individual school must develop an environment in ways that respond to the children and families that it serves. Although all the characteristics of a public such as that described in this section are necessary to create schools that sustain the dignity of children, some may be emphasized more than others. So it may be that a particular school focuses on the intergenerational nature of community, while another creates those midway places for conversation to flourish. It may be that in order to develop deeper connections between students and teachers, one school halves class size, while another school has students remain with the same teacher for two or more years. So while there may be varying combinations of practical ways to develop a public that is rich in making connections, a school concerned with paying attention to the stories of children would address the fundamental concern about how the characteristics of such a public could be met.

EDUCATION AS PAYING ATTENTION TO STORIES

The previous sections of this chapter have talked about creating an environment that would sustain paying attention to the stories of children, as well as looking at the implications of this notion for the quality of caring and attitudes that teachers and other adults involved with children should nurture. I will now turn to what education that pays attention to stories should offer to children's lives. Education as paying attention to the stories or the meaning that children are creating in their lives means valuing their *autonomy* as primary "authors" of their lives, encouraging *reciprocity* in relationships, providing *recognition* for the self, and viewing education as *freedom to imagine* things as they could be otherwise. These four things—authorship, reciprocity, recognition, and freedom to imagine—are necessary components of what it means to pay attention to stories. Before examining them in more detail, I would like to make a general comment about how I characterize this notion of education as paying attention to stories.

Advocating that we pay attention to stories is not a call for the development of a curricula that would include a prepackaged format for storymaking. Such prepackaging would trivialize the notion of paying attention to stories. This would be antithetical to the notion that we must be responsive to the individual making of a life. Rather, advocating for stories would lead us to ask, among other things, about our goals in the classroom—whether or not our schools have enough important adults to listen to the stories of the many children in our midst; whether there are opportunities in teaching to slow down and listen to the voice of one child at a time.

In actuality, we are asking how schools might be different if sustaining dignity and listening to stories were the fundamental commitments. Surely schools that nurture and sustain dignity would pay attention to their organization, methodologies, curricula, and funding, among all the other things schools must worry about. Generally speaking, if the dignity of children in schools is to be nurtured, schools and classes must be smaller, methodologies should be varied, and curricula would take as their starting point a child's natural life experiences. In doing so, schools would create the space for paying attention to the meaning children create in their lives through the vehicle of story. But underlying any and all of these external or structural changes that a school could make are the characteristics and qualities that would permeate the moral relationships between the children and adults in schools.

With this in mind, I will examine the four necessary components that should imbue the nature of how we pay attention to the stories of children and the flourishing of their lives.

AUTHORSHIP

As noted previously, dignity speaks to the need to recognize one another's right to create our own original lives. While still acknowledging the dialogical and contextual nature of creating a story of meaning, each self still retains authorial purpose. Jeffrey Blustein comments on the entwined nature of the relational and autonomous self. He says, "We are not just what we discover ourselves, through some interpretive process, to be. We can, as autonomous choosers of our ends, ask ourselves what kind of person we want to become. While we cannot perhaps directly freely choose our attachments, we can choose to engage in courses of action that we expect to create conditions under which certain attachments will develop."[17] It seems to me that creating the "conditions under which certain attachments will develop" should be a high priority of schools that are committed to paying attention to stories. As the conditions are created, an environment of trust is forged wherein the "unfolding of a lived life," as Coles would have us understand it, could take place. Creating such conditions will allow room for authorship. As Bruner has indicated, the viability of our culture rests on how well we can pay attention to one another's stories. But before we can pay attention to these stories, we have to provide the space for each of us to author them. As we do so, we preserve dignity by allowing persons to be "autonomous choosers of our ends," as Blustein described.

How might this honoring of authorship be recognized by schools? Kohl provides a story that gives us insight into the importance of authorship. The student he describes is not a typical student, but that does not lessen our need to understand the power of authorship and how it can be extended to all children. At the time that Lenny came to school, Kohl was teaching at an alternative high school in Berkeley. Lenny was on the verge of being thrown out of Berkeley High because all he wanted to do was practice his saxophone. He saw school as an interference with that goal. He did not want to do math or English or history. He was labeled a troublemaker and a truant, until finally he was "driven out of the school and into the park—where in fact he practiced his saxophone." (Interestingly, Kohl notes that if Lenny had been a student with economic privilege, it is conceivable that he would be attending a private music academy or having tutors arranged for his educational needs. This evidences the social construction of marginalization or dignity.) So here was Lenny at the doorstep of the alternative high school. Up to this point, Kohl was proud of the fact that the alternative school shaped its curriculum to meet the needs of the students, rather than making students conform to the structure of the school. The school offered many varied courses from which students could choose in order to meet the requirements of English or math. Still, in order to attend and graduate, students had to choose from and attend classes in each subject. But Lenny simply wanted to play his saxophone; he did not want to attend class. Surprising even himself, Kohl feared that allowing Lenny to break the rules and not attend class would open the door for others to do the same. Still, Kohl acknowledged that one of the purposes of the alternative school was to be flexible in meeting student needs even if they were different from that of the traditional educational system.

To be consistent with the mission of the alternative school, and since no other school was willing to take Lenny on his terms, Lenny was admitted to the school. While there, Lenny did not take a class in English, math, or history. In fact, he did not take any classes. Instead, the school was willing to let him determine the scope of his study that focused on music and on contributing to the community of the school. His work was challenging as he did "get piano lessons, learn to read and write music, and practice as long and as well as he could." He also accompanied the school theater and composed and performed his own music in order to receive graduation credit. Lenny worked hard, was involved with his peers and teachers, and learned much that was of critical interest to him. Kohl recounts that Lenny went on to become a successful professional musician. Although critics might think otherwise, responding to the urgency of Lenny's needs did not prevent him from having a productive and successful career. Lenny was one of those rare students who insisted on authoring his own life, and the educators at the alternative school had the wisdom to grant him space to do so.

Although Lenny's case is not typical and the point of the story is not to routinely excuse students from classes because they think they do not want to be there, Kohl provides an insight into the importance of authorship. He says, "Most of us are not as focused or obsessed as Lenny was as a youngster. However, I have never known a child, no matter how superficially unmotivated she or he might seem, whose indifference, hopelessness, or rage did not mask a lively imagination and dreams of challenging work, lasting love, and a fullness of being."[18] Recall the story of Samuel in chapter 2. He *knew* about whales. He was prepared to author his story in school, to share his knowledge and, in so sharing, to continue to create meaning. But the teacher had no time for that. The demands of the curriculum prevented authorship. By contrast, Lenny's school allowed him to claim authorship by bringing the urgency of his own interests, talents, and abilities to this endeavor we call "education."

Without authorship, it is impossible to sustain dignity in the life of a child. Hence, teachers must approach their curriculum with an eye toward allowing children the opportunity to make meaning and articulate meaning and reflect upon meaning. Education cannot be simply an imposition from above, or it risks being shallow and disconnected from the projects of one's life.

RECIPROCITY

Educator Deborah Meier tells a story about asking a group of inner-city youth who had little school success whether they knew anyone who had graduated from college.[19] Expecting to get a response that would point to the lack of educational role models, she was not disappointed. No, these young people said, they knew no one who had graduated from college. "How sad," we think, and "no wonder!" we think, as we bemoan the lack of role models in the lives of our youth. Meier's reaction was similar until she realized that there was something wrong with this story. Since the day these high school students had first set foot in school, some ten, eleven, or twelve years before, they had been in daily contact with whole buildings full of adults who had graduated from college, some with multiple degrees! Why did these young people not count their teachers and principals among their acquaintances, friends, or adults that they knew as persons who had graduated from college? The answer points to the lack of reciprocity.

Too many times, school undermines reciprocity. It creates artificial barriers between teachers and students. These barriers are sometimes structurally created, such as faculty lounges and student cafeterias, but these barriers often are couched within the culture of schools. For example, as a professor, hooks notes that her understanding of "engaged pedagogy" that involves reciprocity sometimes is challenged as not being academically serious enough. She writes:

> Colleagues say to me, "Your students seem to be enjoying themselves, they seem to be laughing whenever I walk by, you seem to be having a good time." And the implication is that you're a good joke-teller, you're a good performer, but no serious teaching is happening. Pleasure in the classroom is feared. If there is laughter, a reciprocal exchange may be taking place. You're laughing, the students are laughing, and someone walks by, looks in and says, "OK, you're able to make them laugh. But so what? Anyone can entertain." They can take this attitude because the idea of reciprocity, or respect, is not ever assumed.[20]

In many educational settings, reciprocity is not encouraged. There is little or no sharing of a teacher's life with students' lives. Perhaps this reflects professionalization with its strict division between work and personal life. But recall my earlier discussion wherein I indicated that school must create a public where lives can flourish. One of the primary ways to develop and sustain such a public is through the sharing of umbilical speech as Green described. The sharing must be reciprocal and accomplished with respect. In sharing parts of their stories, teachers model ways in which they are making sense of their world and the experiences they share with students. In addition, the sharing of such umbilical stories moves beyond the purpose of modeling. It serves to create meaningful connections between teachers and students.

Not only does reciprocity involve challenging the artificial distinction between a teacher's objective stance toward learning and a child's subjective learning, it involves listening with an ear to hear the meaning a child is attempting to make or share. Reciprocity is demonstrated when a teacher steps outside of the classroom and attends a student's piano recital or soccer game. Although a small thing, it demonstrates that the teacher understands that the life of the child extends beyond the walls of the classroom and that who the child is as he or she walks into the classroom is shaped by experiences and relationships outside of the school.

Reciprocity plays a critical role in how one pays attention to stories. Reciprocity prevents dignity from deteriorating to an exaggerated attention on the self. Reciprocity requires that I pay attention to the other in a way that is not just biding time until my own self is the object of attention. It requires that I sincerely take the other into my consideration, a sort of golden rule that emphasizes the intertwined or relational nature of storytelling. It turns us outward and creates a space for the stories of others, as well as our own.

In education that pays attention to stories, reciprocity would be found where teachers and students appropriately share life experiences in the context of learning. It would include teachers sometimes being engaged in aspects of student activities, such as lunch or recess or music, rather than always separating them for their nonacademic activities. For example, many masterful teachers that I have known choose to remain in their rooms and invite their children to eat lunch with them there, or they go out on the playground and play with their kids, or allow their children to stay in at recess and visit as need arises. Reciprocity of this nature would not structurally arrange the world of school into fragments of experience, many different for teacher or children.

Reciprocity nurtures the listening ear and requires teachers to create spaces in their classrooms for individual student voices to be heard. Reciprocity implies a relationship of trust, where respect and dignity are reciprocal between adults and children at school. If children are never to yell at teachers, then reciprocity would require that adults in schools do not yell at students. Reciprocity might encourage students to do some teaching with each other in their classroom or throughout the building. It would encourage a teacher to approach any given curriculum unit realizing that she may have students who know more about the subject than she and find ways to invite student interest and mastery into her own work. It might include children in developing and carrying out discipline strategies, much like peer mediation programs. In these and many other ways, reciprocity is a necessary component in paying attention to stories because it asks of us to consider the other.

Recognition

Recognition requires a focus on the dual aspects of the intimate and the social. On the intimate level, Taylor reminds us of "how much an original identity needs and is vulnerable to the recognition given or withheld by significant others."[21] While the child looks to the intimates of family for recognition from the day of birth, the need for recognition continues as the child develops. It is even posited by some theorists as the most crucial component in therapeutic intervention and personal change.[22] Educators must be concerned about how students in their classes experience recognition. Since education implies growth and change, children must be recognized in a way that conveys a deep positive regard for themselves and others.

Recognition is conveyed through our social relationships. Taylor states that "identities are formed in open dialogue, unshaped by a predefined social script."[23] If the social script is predetermined, then recognition of the self does not occur. What is recognized is the predetermined script or role that the person holds. If teachers and students never step out of their traditional roles, authentic recognition is difficult to achieve. Teachers must see students as the individual children that they are with all that they bring with them into the classroom. Students will develop a deeper connection with their teacher if they have the chance to see his or her humanity and what he or she brings to the classroom from the world "out there." The environment of the classroom must then provide room for unscripted dialogue to occur in order to facilitate moments of recognition.

Recognition also can occur through naming that which was previously unseen. In some cases, teachers have many wonderful opportunities to name abilities, talents, interests for a child. In other situations, a teacher names a discovery, process, or feeling. Here is an example from my own experience in the schools when my younger son was a third grader in Mrs. Bonney's class. I fondly call this vignette "Erin, the Poet."[24]

Once upon a time there was a school, and a third-grade teacher, and a class of twenty-six students. Some could read and some could not. Some children were what you would call "very, very good" and some were, well, "very, very bad." In this class, among all the other children, there was one little girl named Erin. She was one of those children that was not so good. In fact, at the tender age of eight, she

the intimate (with her teacher) and social (with her class) spheres, and when it occurred in the social sphere, it created a type of public that is born from the sharing of umbilical stories.

FREEDOM TO IMAGINE

Freedom is a necessary component of paying attention to the stories and meaning children make in their lives. The sense of freedom that I utilize here is not "freedom from" interference, but rather a sense of "freedom to." Education as paying attention would mean envisioning education itself as the practice of freedom. It would be freedom to know children in their lives and contexts and freedom to imagine. Education as the practice of freedom would nurture imagination, for how could a life story develop if one is not free to imagine how things could be otherwise? Since dignity asks of us to respect one another's right to create our own lives, then in the educational setting, our responsibility would be to provide the resources upon which children can draw to create their lives. A teacher can offer a vast array of ways to envision the world so that the child can draw from deeply varied and rich ways to make sense of the world.

What might education for freedom look like for teachers and students? In *The Dialectic of Freedom*, Maxine Greene indicates that teachers can problematize the everyday or challenge the "flatness of ordinary life." Students can be challenged to endow their world with different meanings. Without recognizing the possibilities for different meanings, students rarely question the "givens" in their daily lives. Without questioning the givens, the project of education with its attention to identity development and meaning making is compromised. Greene describes how the freedom to imagine, or lack thereof, often impacts students' lives. She states:

> Without being "onto something," young people feel little pressure, little challenge. There are no mountains they particularly want to climb, so there are few obstacles with which they feel they need to engage. They may take no heed of neighborhood shapes and events once they have become used to them—even the figure of homelessness, the wanderers who are mentally ill, the garbage-strewn lots, the burned-out buildings. It may be that no one communicates the importance of thinking about them or suggests the need to play with hypothetical alternatives. There may be no sense of identification with people sitting on the benches, with children

hanging around the street corners after dark. There may be no ability to take it seriously, to take it personally. Visible or invisible, the world may not be problematized; no one aches to break through a horizon, aches in the presence of the question itself. So there are no tensions, no desires to reach beyond.[25]

The freedom to imagine is the freedom to envision things in new ways. It is the freedom do engage with the "everydayness" of the world and pose new questions of possibility.

At times, one engages with students who have been sufficiently marginalized so that their defiant attitude stands in the way of their learning. Kohl would call this defiance "creative maladjustment," as a reasonable response to marginalization. Education that offers freedom to imagine has something to offer such students. After hearing how the student makes sense of his or her world (perhaps many times over), a teacher can invite such a student to consider other ways of making sense of the experience the student has had. Sometimes freedom to imagine entails naming that for which the student has no name (as with Erin, the poet), and other times, it is simply an opening of possibilities. Alternatively, freedom to imagine, especially in adolescent years, would do as Maxine Greene describes. It would "identify the gaps between what is and what is longed for, what (if the sphere of freedom is ever developed) will some day come to be."[26] Adolescence is a time for such longing, and education that pays attention to stories would help students fill the gap that Greene identifies by calling upon other stories of possibility and helping students to articulate their own.

In order to be the type of school that draws upon freedom to imagine as a way to pay attention to stories of children, schools must be about more than preparing students for the status quo. By its very nature, imagination challenges how a given is perceived. Hence, teaching assists children to imagine how things could be otherwise, whether it be in science, literature, history, or their own lives. The very act of hearing others' stories is a way to impress upon young minds that experience can be otherwise. This is what Maxine Greene challenges us to do. She states that "freedom signifies—the freedom to alter situations by reinterpreting them and, by so doing, seeing oneself as a person in a new perspective. Once that happens, there are new beginnings, new actions to take in the world."[27] The image this provides for me is one of expansion and growth and that signifies education.

These four components interact with and depend upon each other as educators pay attention to the stories of children. Each of the four components can be fulfilled and put into practice in many different ways. The practices of various schools and teachers may be varied as they address these elements. Yet education that pays attention to stories in order to sustain the dignity of children must in some way incorporate each of these four notions of *authorship, reciprocity, recognition,* and *freedom to imagine.*

Reprise: No Small Matter

As Richard Wright cautioned, when we choose not to pay attention to the "best and deepest things of heart and mind," we are truly tossing away what it means to be human. This surely cannot be the choice we would make for ourselves or our children and should not be the choice we make for anyone. Creating spaces and opportunities for lives to be told as narratives incorporates attention to contextuality and the relational nature of the self. As stories are heard, dignity is affirmed in the process of telling (I am here!) as well as in the process of listening (You are a part of this whole!) Adrienne Rich states that "when someone with the authority of a teacher, say, describes the world and you are not in it, there is a moment of psychic disequilibrium, as if you looked into a mirror and saw nothing."[28] Taking seriously the notion of dignity would mean we would share a commitment to preventing the moment Rich described from occurring in the lives of children within our schools. Perhaps we would even be prepared to help name the world to include the child, as in Erin's case, when a story is so fragile that it barely exists at all. In other cases, it would mean expanding the possibilities so that children could name their own world.

Take away the understanding of the narrative construction of the self, and one loses understanding the richness and depth of human development and cultural resources. Take away the language of a culture, and one loses the carrier of meaning. In schools, take away the identity-making focus of education and there are only marginalized persons left, marginal to the task at hand, cut-off from the task of growth and development, and alienated from the institutional structure charged with their care for a predominant portion of their pre-adult lives. To remedy this? Given the narrative nature of the self, we should pay attention to what those narratives carry, that is, the meaning and context of a life. We should pay attention to the quality of human relationships, develop rich and full languages, and hold as a priority the identity-making features of the educational institution. We should pay attention to stories and how they connect persons to their cultures and society at large. In this way, as identity can be honored, dignity can be sustained. Overcoming marginalization by sustaining dignity entails paying attention to the stories of individuals, since all these function to create a life.

CONCLUSION

What I am proposing and where I am pointing our attention do not provide an easy answer to the various educational problems our society has identified. In addressing responsibilities that are essentially moral in nature, this work addresses what is deeply significant, but does not attempt either comprehensive or simply applied answers. One of my concerns in writing a book such as this that does not claim to provide a clear-cut answer is that some may be tempted to set aside my argument as inconsequential for these reasons. To anyone so tempted, I offer the following considerations.

First, the argument that education that pays attention to stories can sustain and nurture dignity, and, in turn, help children's lives flourish is not an idea or concept that can be captured in a curriculum or distilled into a methodology. It cannot be transported like a template onto schools. Rather, my argument requires that those of us involved in education and children's lives critically reflect upon the quality of the relationships we have with children, as teachers, as parents, as administrators, as researchers. This type of reflection is challenging. It is deeply personal, and the measure of its success is also often very personal. Sometimes the changes in the lives of one's students are apparent to many. Teachers who understand that education must pay attention to the stories of children often are perceived as masterful teachers. This work attempts to describe what it is that makes them so. Yet at other times, the changes in students' lives are known only in that small community of the classroom or only to the student and teacher. And in other cases, the impact of such attention may be recognized only years after a student has passed through the influence of such a teacher. Hence, one cannot judge the moral consequences of this argument with a statement such as, "The proof is in the pudding!" This pudding is not quantifiable, and yet it is fundamental to education properly understood.

Second, the argument set forth in this book does not purport to be a "total" answer to our educational ills. I would be leery of any educational proposal that claims to have such a sweeping answer, whether it be cast as the privatization of the public schools or cooperative learning as a methodology or constructivist teaching. Attending to the stories of children, while necessary, is in any case not sufficient to a good education. Rather, it forms the basis of an education that can be powerful as we pay attention to the lives of children.

Third, the argument I have set forth asks a lot of all of us involved in the education of young people. It especially asks a lot of teachers and principals, custodians and cooks, and those who are with our children on almost a daily basis. With all the demands placed on teachers today, it is not my intent simply to create another "solution" that they will have to import and implement. Instead, it asks teachers to reflect on their own work in the school setting, to challenge and question the givens of the educational system, and to look carefully at the nature of the relationships among teachers and students and schools. The argument I develop herein does not impugn the motivations of the countless teachers who are giving their best to their teaching. Rather, it asks each of us involved with children to imagine, for a moment, how things might be otherwise in the schools we have created for children.

Given that I address the moral character of education and the relationships therein, accepting the argument I have set forth suggests that as educators, we have the following fundamental responsibilities.

Initially, we need to be thoughtfully reflective about the quality of the teaching and relationships that occur in our classroom and school. It is important to ask of the ways we teach, Does this help the lives of the children in my class flourish? or Does this nurture and sustain the dignity of the children in my class? in the many ways this book has suggested. Teaching so that the lives of our students might flourish asks of us to come to know the lives of our students. We come to know their lives as we create room for their stories.

Subsequently, we need to nurture the habit of questioning recommended educational practice, whether it be a traditional style or the latest educational fad. In other words, we should let our imaginations consider other possibilities. That means I thoughtfully ask of my own practice, Why do I do it this way? and Who benefits from the way I "do" education? and What are other possibilities? and Who might be left out? Knowing why we teach what and how we do is an empowering position for a teacher. It allows us to bring ourselves to the process—to bring our passions, our hopes, our own imaginations.

What both of these basic responsibilities have in common is that they require us to know ourselves and to know our students. As we bring ourselves and invite our students to bring themselves into our classrooms, we are creating moral communities of teachers and learners. As discussed throughout this book, creating such communities is at the crux of teaching for understanding, of enlarging the meaning of our storied lives, and realizing the promises of growth that Dewey envisioned. This book invites us to consider and respond to these and similar questions with practices that affirm the dignity of children. That does not preclude additional instrumental or educative reasons from occupying a teacher's mind, but it places a concern for the dignity and flourishing of children's lives at the base of our educational decision making.

For some, accepting the argument presented here will require a change of heart toward how we think of students, parents, and ourselves as educators. We cannot see them as adversaries. We must be patient and persevering. Changing how we think about our relationships with children, how we teach, and how we are in relationships with others is at the crux of this discussion of dignity. We need to understand that we can make a difference in the lives of children and that in order to truly educate, to move them from the margins to the heart of educational growth, we must pay attention to the stories of their lives.

NOTES

1. IMAGINING EDUCATION

1. John I. Goodlad, *What Schools Are For* (Phi Delta Kappa Educational Foundation, 1994), 26.

2. For a description of the Tier 3 interdisciplinary synthesis course requirement for all seniors, see Ohio University Catalog, Athens, Ohio, 1995–96, 343.

3. Thomas Green, "Unwrapping the Ordinary: Philosophical Projects," *American Journal of Education* (November 1991): 84–105.

4. I am indebted to Dr. Deborah Kerdeman (University of Washington, Seattle) who developed a competing social values framework for analyzing educational dilemmas.

5. Robert Bellah, Richard Madsen, William Sullivan, Ann Swidler, and Steven Tipton, *Habits of the Heart: Individualism and Commitment in American Life* (New York: Harper and Row, 1986). See also Alexis de Tocqueville, *Democracy in America* (New York: Harper and Row, 1969), and Eva T. H. Braun, *Paradoxes of Education in a Republic* (Chicago: University of Chicago Press, 1979).

6. Bruce C. Hafen, "Developing Student Expression through Institutional Authority: Public Schools as Mediating Structures," *The Ohio State Law Journal* 48 (1987): 728–29.

7. Ibid., 667.

8. Ibid.

9. Ibid., 729.

10. George Wood, *Schools That Work* (New York: Plume Books, 1992), xiii–xxiii.

11. Stephen Toulmin, *The Uses of Argument* (Cambridge: Cambridge University Press), 96.

12. Green, "Unwrapping," 88.

13. John Searle, "How to Derive 'Ought' from 'Is,'" *The Philosophical Review* 73 (January 1964).

2. No Small Matter

1. John Goodlad, *A Place Called School* (New York: McGraw-Hill, 1984). For a discussion of the multiple demands placed on schools by various sources, see especially chapter 2, "We Want It All."

2. "Girl Dies; 7 Held in Ballard Shooting," *Seattle Times*, March 24, 1994, Section A1.

3. "Public Is Frustrated with Schools," *Seattle Post-Intelligencer*, September 9, 1994, Section B1.

4. For a discussion of how and why culturally diverse children do not have equal educational outcomes, see the following: Lisa Delpit, *Other People's Children: Cultural Conflict in the Classroom* (New York: The New Press, 1995); James Comer, "Educating Poor Minority Children," *Scientific American* 259, no. 5 (November 1988): 42–28; Geneva Gay, "Achieving Educational Equality through Curriculum Desegregation," *Phi Delta Kappan* 72, no. 1 (September 1990): 56–62; Harold Hodgkin, "Reform versus Reality," *Phi Delta Kappan* 73, no. 1 (September 1991): 8–16; and Marian Wright Edelman, *Portrait of Inequality: Black and White Children in America* (Washington D.C.: The Children's Defense Fund, 1980).

5. For a discussion of how we look to the schools to solve our pressing social problems, see David Tyack and Elisabeth Hansot, "Conflict and Consensus in American Public Education," *Daedalus*, 110, no. 3 (Summer 1981)): 13. See also Melvin Lazerson, *An Education of Value* (Cambridge: Cambridge University Press, 1985), see especially chapter 1, pp. 3–22. See also Christopher Lasch, *The Revolt of the Elites and the Betrayal of Democracy* (New York: W. W. Norton & Company, 1995), especially chapter 8, "The Common Schools: Horace Mann and the Assault on the Imagination."

6. For example, in *American Education* (New York: Longman, 1991), Joel Spring states: "It is easier to give a health course than to change job conditions, improve urban environments, or manipulate family traditions. Of even greater importance is the fact that the school is less threatening than such direct changes" (14). See also Valerie Polakow, *Lives on the Edge: Single Mothers and Their Children in the Other America* (Chicago: University of

Chicago Press, 1993), especially chapter 9, for a description of how poverty and other encompassing social issues impact the success of children in schools.

7. In this regard, see John Goodlad, "We Want It All," *A Place Called School* (New York: McGraw-Hill), 33–60. His findings suggest that parents generally give less than satisfactory marks to schools as a whole, but are more than willing to give satisfactory marks to their own child's schools. Additionally, see Patricia Graham, *S.O.S.: Sustain Our Schools* (New York: Hill and Wang, 1992). Graham documents actual improvements made in education. See also David Berliner and Bruce Biddle, *The Manufactured Crisis* (Reading, MA: Addison-Wesley, 1995) for a discussion of how the effectiveness of American education has been distorted to create a public sense of crisis in the American schools.

8. Professor Thomas Green identified this distinction in educational reform and research foci during a College of Education colloquium discussion at the University of Washington, May 2, 1995, Seattle, WA.

9. Alfie Kohn, "Choices for Children: Why and How to Let Students Decide," in *Phi Delta Kappan* 75, no. 1 (September 1993): 12.

10. See Jonathan Kozol, *Savage Inequalities: Children in America's Schools* (New York: Crown Publishers, 1991), for a description of the wretched physical conditions of public schools in poor neighborhoods where many children must attend.

11. "Children in America's Schools," a Bill Moyer special, PBS.

12. See Peter Cookson and Catherine Persell, *Preparing for Power: America's Elite Boarding Schools* (New York: Basic Books, 1995), and Robert Coles, *Privileged Ones: The Well-off and the Rich in America* (Boston: Little, Brown, 1977). Both books report the psychological and emotional strain placed on kids when family expectations reflect rigid class expectations.

13. I am also concerned with the students who simply accept the traditional role of student and digest all the given information in order to make good grades or be successful as defined external to themselves. These students as well may be marginalized from the transformative power of educative experiences. Rather than explore this, we generally celebrate the success of school in the lives of these hard-working, but compliant students.

14. Ira Shor, *Empowering Education: Critical Teaching for Social Change* (Chicago: University of Chicago Press, 1992).

15. Jerome Bruner, *Acts of Meaning* (Cambridge, MA: Harvard University Press, 1990), 12–13.

16. Joel Spring, *American Education* (New York: Longman, 1991). See chapter 1, "The Purposes of Public Schooling."

17. Many schools provide a varying continuum of services such as these and consider them appropriate to the mission of education. For example, most have school nurses, a counselor/psychologist, and a school breakfast and lunch program. Some high schools have health clinics. For a discussion of an enriched role for these extra services, see Jane Roland Martin, *The Schoolhome: Rethinking Schools for Changing Families* (Cambridge,

MA: Harvard University Press, 1992), and Sharon Quint, *Homeless Children: A Working Model for America's Public Schools* (New York: Teachers College Press, 1994).

18. For a description of the research work and practice of utilizing diverse historical, cultural, and autobiographical stories in the classroom, see the following: Lucy McCormick Calkins, *Living between the Lines* (Portsmouth, NH: Heinemann, 1991); Carol Witherell and Nel Noddings, eds., *Stories Lives Tell: Narrative and Dialogue in Education* (New York: Teachers College Press, 1991); Kieran Egan, *Teaching as Story-Telling: An Alternative Approach to Teaching and Curriculum in the Elementary School* (Chicago: University of Chicago Press, 1986); M. Fleming and J. McGinnis, eds., *Portraits: Biography and Autobiography in the Secondary School* (Urbana: National Council of Teachers of English, 1985); M. O. Tunnel and R. Ammon, eds., *The Story of Ourselves: Teaching History through Children's Literature* (Portsmouth, NH: Heinemann, 1993).

19. From the preamble of the *Professional Standards and Code of Ethics* of the National Education Association.

3. IGNORING THE DEMANDS OF DIGNITY

1. This claim refers to the largest uninterrupted portion of the child's day (excluding weekends). For example, a child's day at school goes from approximately 8:00 A.M. to 3:00 P.M. While that child may have close to the same amount of hours at home before bed, these hours are usually filled with mixed activities, sometimes little adult contact, less one-on-one adult contact, a lot of TV, or other activities that are not necessarily sustained in nature and in the company and supervision of adults.

2. John Goodlad, *What Schools Are For* (Phi Delta Kappa Educational Foundation, 1994), 37.

3. It is important to note that how one creates a life, identifies its component parts and how one stands in relation to others is culturally influenced. No doubt this work, like every other, is informed by deep cultural assumptions. While culture may provide the parameters of how one creates a life and thinks about it, I would argue that it is still the case that each culture understands that we have lives, that we are individuals (defined in varying degrees), and that we do make meaning. It is to these processes that my book speaks, acknowledging that culture plays a significant role in how we experience all these processes.

4. John Dewey, "My Pedagogic Creed," in Reed, Ronald, and Tony Johnson, eds. *Philosophical Documents in Education*. (New York: Longman Publishers USA; 1996), 113.

5. For a discussion of "Education and Growth," see John Dewey, *Democracy and Education* (New York: The Free Press, 1916/1944), 41–53.

6. Herbert Kohl, *I Won't Learn from You and Other Thoughts on Creative Maladjustment* (New York: The New Press, 1994), 26–27.

7. Anthony Kwame Appiah draws a distinction regarding identity making that is similar to the distinction I make here with marginalization. He indicates that there are two types of identity: collective and personal. The collective involves identifying oneself with the broad social categories that define oneself, such as male or female, African American or European American, homosexual or heterosexual, etc. These categories define one's identity to an extent, because they possess a social meaning. This intersects with personal identity, which, among other things, speaks of the personal characteristics that one uses to describe oneself, such as witty, serious, personable, smart, etc. Roughly speaking, marginalization that occurs in the realm of collective identity is stereotypic marginalization. Marginalization that occurs in the realm of personal identity is psycho-social. For a futher discussion of Appiah's distinction, see Anthony Kwame Appiah in Charles Taylor, *Multiculturalism: Examining the Politics of Recognition* (Princeton: Princeton University Press, 1994).

8. For a discussion of the stereotypic marginalization of students in our nation's public schools, see the following books: Michael Apple, *Official Knowledge: Democratic Education in a Conservative Age* (New York: Routledge, 1993); Lisa Delpit, *Other People's Children: Cultural Conflict in the Classroom* (New York: The New Press, 1995); Jonathan Kozol, *Savage Inequalities: Children in America's Schools* (New York: Crown Publishers, 1991); Valerie Polakow, *Lives on the Edge: Single Mothers and Their Children in the Other America* (Chicago: University of Chicago Press, 1993); and Lois Weiss, *Beyond Silenced Voices: Class, Race, and Gender in United States Schools* (Albany: State University of New York Press, 1993).

9. My contention here is not that the children come with deficits, but that practices in our public schools discriminate and marginalize along the lines of race, class, gender, and ability. My view more closely reflects the "cultural difference" paradigm which indicates that "ethnic minority youths fail to achieve in school not because they have culturally deprived cultures but because their cultures are different from the culture of the school." This is in contrast to the "cultural deprivation" paradigm that sees the "major problem as the culture of the students rather than the culture of the school." See James A. Banks, *An Introduction to Multicultural Education* (Boston: Allyn and Bacon, 1994), 48–50.

10. Patricia Hill Collins, *Black Feminist Thought: Knowledge, Consciousness, and the Politics of Empowerment* (New York: Routledge, 1991), 68–69.

11. Sharon Quint, *Schooling Homeless Children: A Working Model for America's Public Schools* (New York: Teachers College Press, 1994), 34–35.

12. See Polakow, 187.

13. I note here that "difference" itself need not necessarily result in marginalization. This notion of stereotypical marginalization speaks to how individuals and groups can be dismissed by utilizing a distinction of difference. In such a negative usage, the chosen category of difference simply becomes the avenue for making a moral dismissal of an individual or a

group. Alternatively, when viewed in a positive sense, the notion of difference can lead to respect of others and their right to define their own lives in the context of cultural heritage.

14. See Polakow, especially chapter 7, "The Classroom Worlds of At-Risk Children: Five Portraits," and chapter 8, "Poor Children's Pedagogy: The Construction of At-Risk Students."

15. Polakow, 135.

16. The ability to ascribe meaning to one's own identity is not a superficial concern. Such a concern has driven changes in the labels we do give. For example, in providing education for all children, Public Law 94–142 was enacted and entitled "Education for Handicapped Persons Act." This law since has been revised and retitled "Individuals with Disabilities Educational Act" (IDEA), precisely because the advocates for persons with disabilities want to make the point that these children must be seen as individual human beings first and then as persons with particular disabilities. Using the former label and classifying an individual as a "handicapped person" had the tendency to make the person invisible and the label or category stand for what that person was.

17. John Jay Bonstingl, *Introduction to the Social Sciences* (Boston: Allyn and Bacon, 1980), 290.

18. Kwame Anthony Appiah, in Charles Taylor, *Multiculturalism: Examining the Politics of Recognition* (Princeton: Princeton University Press, 1994), 162–63.

19. Collins, 94.

20. James Scott, *Domination and the Arts of Resistance* (New Haven: Yale University Press, 1990), 31.

21. Calkins, 21.

22. Ibid., 30.

23. Peter W. Cookson, Jr., and Caroline Hodges Persell, *Preparing for Power: America's Elite Boarding Schools* (New York: Basic Books, Inc., 1985), 25.

24. Andrei Codrescu, *Zombification* (New York: Picador, 1994), 35.

25. Paulo Freire, *Pedagogy of the Oppressed* (New York: Continuum, 1990), 58.

26. It is encouraging to note that middle schools and some high schools are restructuring their educational communities to serve more closely the needs of the developing student. In this regard, schools are limiting size by creating schools within schools, creating "family" groupings of students and teachers, having a team of teachers work with a cohort of students throughout the time they are at the school, and providing flexibility in scheduling by dismantling bell schedules. In this regard, see the following: Carnegie Council on Adolescent Development, *Turning Points: Preparing American Youth for the Twenty-First Century* (Washington, DC: Carnegie Corporation, 1989); Nancy L. Ames and Edward Miller, *Changing Middle Schools: How to Make Schools Work for Young Adolescents* (San Francisco: Jossey-Bass, 1994); Anne C. Lewis, *Making It in the Middle: The Why and How of Excellent Schools for Young Urban Adolescents* (New York: The Edna McConnel Clark Foundation, 1990).

27. It is important to note that these two forms of marginalization are often interactive in nature. Hence, one might think that stereotypic marginalization also puts the development of the self at risk, but this occurs only insofar that resources for the individual become so scarce that they have nothing upon which to draw for identity development and meaning-making activities. Then the individual faces both forms of marginalization. This distinction will be discussed later in this chapter.

28. Kohl, *I Won't Learn*, 1–2.

29. Martin Luther King, Jr., *I Have a Dream: Writing and Speeches that Changed the World*, James M. Washington, ed. (San Francisco: Harper San Francisco, 1992), 33.

30. Scott, 18.

31. Ibid., 25–28, 119.

32. Bell hooks, *Yearning: Race, Gender and Cultural Politics* (Boston: South End Press, 1990).

33. Richard Wright, *Black Boy* (New York: Harper and Row, 1937/1966), 284.

34. Kohl, *I Won't Learn*, 28.

35. This does not mean that every child who misbehaves should be understood as resisting marginalization. Nor does it mean that even if the misbehavior is a response to marginalization, then it should be overlooked. Understanding that misbehavior is sometimes a resistance to marginalization in schools does not preclude judgment about what is appropriate and what is not. What it does require is that before students are labeled, dismissed, disciplined, etc., the adults involved in their lives should ask themselves and the student about the meaning of those actions. For instance, ask, Why is this student behaving in such a way? Too often we have answered, "Because he is Black, she lives in poverty, he has a single parent, she has attention deficit disorder. Oh, I know what this is a case of. . . . " In this way, we dismiss the responsibility to look at the institution or ourselves as causes. We place the blame on the child.

36. Scott, 206–217.

37. Ibid., 215.

38. Herbert Kohl, *36 Children* (New York: New American Library, 1967/1988).

4. THE ROLE OF DIGNITY

1. Vivian Paley, *The Boy Who Would Be a Helicopter* (Cambridge, MA: Harvard University Press, 1990), xi.

2. Daniel Pekarsky, "Dehumanization and Education," *Teachers College Record* 84, no. 2, (Winter 1982): 339–53.

3. Shor, 12.

4. Charles Taylor, *The Ethics of Authenticity* (Cambridge, MA: Harvard University Press, 1991), 28–29.

5. Ibid., 40.

6. Carol Gould, *Rethinking Democracy* (New York: Cambridge University Press), 25.

7. Maxine Greene, *The Dialectic of Freedom* (New York: Teachers College Press, 1988), 70.

8. For a discussion of the reasons why keeping a school small is fundamental to achieving additional goals related to helping all students succeed, refer to Deborah Meier, *The Power of Their Ideas: Lessons for America from a Small School in Harlem* (Boston: Beacon Press, 1995). See especially chapter 6 where she discusses six reasons why smallness is critical to significant school change. Briefly, these are the following: (1) small schools allow participatory democracy to take place in a way that is not unmangeable; (2) small schools provide faculty access to one another's work and can facilitate a collective sense of responsibility; (3) small schools create the space where teachers truly come to know how a student works and thinks; (4) small schools offer safety in that everyone is known to one another; (5) small schools encourage accountability to parents and the community as they provide accessibility to the school and faculty; and (6) small schools create a culture where students and adults can truly interact and students can benefit from immersion in a place where the community and adult influence can counteract those messages of hopelessness and disconnectedness.

9. Appiah, in Taylor, *Ethics of Authenticity*, 151.

10. For a discussion of how culture influences the development of the self, see Alan Roland, *In Search of Self in India and Japan: Towards a Cross-Cultural Psychology* (Princeton: Princeton University Press, 1988). While recognizing different structures of the self ("I-self," "We-self," and "Spiritual self,"), Roland's psychiatric work in the United States, India, and Japan demonstrates how the influence of culture determines the varying emphases on each one of the different structures of the self.

11. Taylor, *Ethics of Authenticity*, 32–33.

12. "Refugees Stories Project," Public Display, Seattle Central Community College, 1994.

13. Jerome Bruner, *Acts of Meaning* (Cambridge, MA: Harvard University Press, 1990), 89.

14. Ibid., 99–138. See especially chapter 4, "Autobiography and Self."

15. George C. Rosenwald and Richard L. Ochberg, *Storied Lives: The Cultural Politics of Self-Understanding* (New Haven: Yale University Press, 1992), 5.

16. Donald Polkinghorne, *Narrative Knowing and the Human Sciences* (Albany: State University of New York Press, 1988), 150.

17. James R. Price III and Charles H. Simpkinson in Charles and Anne Simpkinson, eds., *Sacred Stories: A Celebration of the Power of Story to Transform and Heal* (San Francisco: HarperCollins, 1993), 12–13.

18. Alasdair MacIntyre, *After Virtue* (Notre Dame: University of Notre Dame Press, 1981). See chapter 15 in particular, "The Virtues, the Unity of a Human Life and the Concept of a Tradition," 204–225.

19. Richard Rorty, *Contingency, Irony, and Solidarity* (Cambridge: Cambridge University Press, 1989), xv, 189.

20. Ibid., 93.

21. Ibid., 109.

22. Seyla Benhabib, *Situating the Self* (Cambridge, MA: Harvard University Press, 1993), 7.

23. Ibid., 7.

24. Ibid., 29–32.

25. Ibid., 8.

26. Rorty, 51.

27. As will be noted in chapter 6, there are ways that paying attention to meaning can dominate the story of a child. This kind of attention would not sustain dignity, but would marginalize children as described in this chapter. In addition, the activity of paying attention to the meaning children are making should not be construed as having to know all that the child is thinking, dreaming, hoping, etc. Such an invasion into the private space of the child would also be domination. Rather, the point made here relates to the appropriate relationships that occur in education.

28. Paley, 21.

29. Ibid., 12.

30. See Martin, *The Schoolhome,* and Nel Noddings, Caring: *A Feminine Approach to Ethics and Moral Education* (Berkeley: The University of California Press, 1984), especially chapter 8, "Moral Education," 171–201.

31. Eamonn Callan, "Finding a Common Voice," *Educational Theory*, 42 no. 4: 436.

5. THE POWER OF STORY

1. Rosenwald and Ochberg, 1.

2. Paley, xi.

3. Richard Rodriguez, *Hunger of Memory* (New York: Bantam Books, 1982), 187.

4. John Dewey, *Experience and Education* (New York: Macmillan Publishing Company, 1938), 62.

5. Martha Nussbaum, *Love's Knowledge: Essays on Philosophy and Literature* (New York: Oxford Un iversity Press, 1990), 7, 23–24.

6. It might be helpful to imagine what it would be like for a child *not* to pay attention to his or her own story. In this regard, I have worked with children who have been abused in one form or another, and the story they play out is often the story of their abusers, rather than their own. For example, recall the short story by D. H. Lawrence, "The Rocking Horse Winner." In this story, the little boy was so preoccupied with solving his mother's problem that he simply adopted her story. In the end, it destroyed any hope for him to have his own. One could argue that the story the child adopts is

his or her own no matter what, but recall that the requirement of authenticity as defined by Taylor requires that the story represent one's own way of being in the world. This would preclude having one's story dominated by that of another.

7. Benhabib, *Situating the Self*, 8.

8. Milbrey McLaughlin, Merita Irby, Juliet Langman, *Urban Sanctuaries* (San Francisco: Jossey-Bass, 1994).

9. For a discussion of the "ethic of care" that pays attention to the particular and the contextual, see Carol Gilligan, *In a Different Voice* (Cambridge, MA: Harvard University Press, 1982); Jane Roland Martin, *The Schoolhome: Rethinking Schools for Changing Families* (Cambridge, MA: Harvard University Press, 1992); and Nel Noddings, *Caring: A Feminine Approach to Ethics and Moral Education* (Berkeley: The University of California Press, 1984).

10. Rosenwald and Ochberg, 9.

11. Howard Brody, *Stories of Sickness* (New Haven: Yale University Press, 1987), 5.

12. Eva Hoffman, *Lost in Translation* (New York: Penguin Books, 1989), 143.

13. Brody, 45.

14. Robert Coles, *The Call of Stories: Teaching and the Moral Imagination* (Boston: Houghton-Mifflin, 1989). See especially chapter 1, "Stories and Theories," 1–30.

15. For a discussion of how narratives might be judged better or worse than another, see Rosenwald and Ochberg, especially "Reflections on Self-Understanding," 265–89.

16. Brody, 27.

17. See Thomas Kuhn, *The Structure of Scientific Revolutions* (Chicago: University of Chicago Press, 1970).

18. Paley, 11.

19. Brody, 14.

20. Jacquelyn Wiersma, "Karen: The Transforming Story," in Rosenwald and Ochberg, *Storied Lives*, 200.

21. Rodriguez, 187.

22. Paley, 21.

23. Rodriguez, 190.

24. Rosenwald and Ochberg, 60.

25. Ibid., 61.

26. Rene Arcilla, "How Can the Misanthrope Learn? Philosophy for Education" in *Philosophy of Education 1994* (Urbana, IL: Philosophy of Education Society, 1995), 353.

27. Scott, 25.

28. Bruner, 96.

29. Ibid., 109.

30. Wiersma, 196.

6. Story and Our Moral Responsibility

1. Adam Zachary Newton, *Narrative Ethics* (Cambridge: Harvard University Press, 1995), 13.

2. Taylor, *Ethics of Authenticity*, 29.

3. Polakow, 141–44.

4. Hoffman, 29.

5. Paley, 5.

6. Hans-Georg Gadamer, *Truth and Method* (New York: Continuum, 1993), 268.

7. Jacob Neusner, *Telling Tales: Making Sense of Christian and Judaic Nonsense* (Louisville: Westminster Press, 1993).

8. What is deeply troubling is that we may be at a point in our own society where we truly are unable to resonate with others' experiences because we simply do not have enough in common. In some instances we may have lost a large enough base of common experience that it is very difficult to find these resonating lived experiences. Then our task is not only to facilitate the hearing of one another's stories, but it is also the larger matter of ensuring that we have cultural experience that is common. Some of the implications of this are that we must question and act upon an economy that creates such extremes in lifestyles that persons are insulated from knowing what struggling to meet the demands of daily life are like.

9. Neusner; see chapter 6, "From Doctrine to Imagination: A Different Kind of Dialogue," for a discussion of how distinct cultural stories can form an authentic dialogue between two diverse groups.

10. Sara Ruddick, *Maternal Thinking: Toward a Politics of Peace* (Boston: Beacon Press, 1995), 11.

11. Brody, 10.

12. Ibid., 8.

13. Scott, 168.

14. Bell hooks, *Teaching to Transgress: Education as the Practice of Freedom* (New York: Routledge, 1994), 74–75.

15. Paulo Freire, *Pedagogy of the Oppressed* (New York: Continuum, 1990), 67.

16. Hooks, *Transgress*, 21.

17. This simplified representation is for heuristic purposes. It is obvious that each of our stories is told and created by the multiple voices of our families and cultures. In like manner, the individual as listener does not listen with singular "ears," but hears impinged by various cultural voices. An issue related to identifying a teller and a listener occurs when the individual who has the story to tell is physically or emotionally incapable of telling her or his story. In this case, intervention is required in order to ascertain a story. The ethical considerations for the one who intervenes as "voice" are complex, indeed. This issue would be interesting addressed by those with expertise in the field of education of persons with disabilities.

18. Hoffman, 279.

19. Taylor, *Ethics of Authenticity*, 33.

20. Ibid., 40–41.

21. Brody, 188.

22. Ibid., 182.

23. Ibid., 160.

24. Richard Wright, *Black Boy* (New York: Harper and Row, 1966), 284.

25. Paley, 62.

26. Ramon Gutierrez, *When Jesus Came, the Corn Mothers Went Away* (Stanford: Stanford University Press, 1991).

27. Freire, 57–74.

28. Megan Boler, The Risks of Empathy: Interrogating Multiculturalism's Gaze," in *Philosophy of Education 1994* (Urbana, IL: Philosophy of Education Society, 1995), 208–219.

29. Bruner, 96–97.

7. Paying Attention to Stories

1. Hooks, *Transgress*, 2–3.

2. We must be careful what conclusions we draw from this example. Does this mean we need only advocate deeper moral relationships and forget about funding education? After all, this school probably existed with little money. Certainly, it is not my conclusion that more equitable funding should not be pursued. This school existed in spite of the lack of funding because of the nature of the community that existed there. Paying more attention to the moral obligation we have in schooling should lead to more equitable funding, not to an abdication of our fiscal responsibilities.

3. Hooks, *Transgress*, 3–4.

4. If this suggestion is taken seriously, it implies that teacher education preparation programs must consciously spend time with their preservice teachers in answering some foundational questions such as What is education? What is its goal? How and why do I teach this way and not that way? What is the relationship between school and society? Who am I, as a teacher, and what unique gifts do I bring to the classroom? From my experience, most teacher education preparation programs spend only a little time on these most fundamental questions in favor of more time for methodology, curriculum, and classroom management coursework.

5. George S. Counts, *Dare the School Build a New Social Order?* (Carbondale: Southern Illinois University Press, 1932), 50–52.

6. Kohl, 38.

7. Thomas S. Green, "Public Speech," *18th Annual DeGarmo Lecture, The Society of Professors of Education* (San Francisco: Caddo Gap Press, 1993), 5.

8. Ibid., 14.

9. Ibid., 11.

10. Green is not oblivious to the challenges of creating public speech. He identifies three "fallacies of public speech" as follows: (1) "Fallacies of Role and Position" where speech is summarily dismissed because of who one is, rather than what one says, (2) "Fallacies of Explanation," where speech is ignored in favor of explaining why one might be saying such and such, and (3) "Fallacies of Misplaced Discourse," where the speech that is criticized is from an auxiliary source, rather than from the speaker him or herself. See Green, "Public Speech" pp. 15–18 for a full discussion of these challenges.

11. Green, "Public Speech," 11.

12. Polkinghorne, 15–16.

13. I recognize that stories may also be used to exclude or dominate others. The "Auditory Principle" guards against this possibility by suggesting that each story must be listened to in a special way. Inclusivity or the principle of "Egalitarian Reciprocity" that Benhabib recommends also mediates against a tendency to use stories to dominate. This requires that all voices participate.

14. Hooks, *Yearning*, 33.

15. Christopher Lasch, *The Revolt of the Elites and the Betrayal of Democracy* (New York: W. W. Norton and Company, 1995), 206.

16. Ibid., 120, 122. For Oldenburg's original discussion of third places, see Ray Oldenburg, *The Great Good Places: Cafes, Coffee Shops, Community Centers, Beauty Parlors, General Stores, Bars, Hangouts and How They Get You through the Day* (New York: Paragon House, 1989.)

17. Jeffrey Blustein, *Care and Commitment: Taking the Personal Point of View* (Oxford: Oxford University Press, 1991), 4–5.

18. Kohl, 71–73.

19. Deborah Meier, "Transforming Schools Into Powerful Communities." *Teachers College Record*, v94, n3 (Spring 1993): 654–58.

20. Hooks, *Transgress*, 145.

21. Taylor, *Multiculturalism*, 49.

22. Carl Rogers, *A Way of Being* (Boston: Houghton-Mifflin, 1980). Rogers argued that therapy could not be effective until certain conditions were met in the relationship between therapist and client. One of the conditions fundamental to therapeutic change is that of "unconditional positive regard." See especially "The Foundations of a Person-Centered Approach," 113–36.

23. Taylor, *Multiculturalism*, 49.

24. I am indebted to Joyce Bonney for sharing her reflections about this experience as the teacher of this wonderful classroom.

25. Maxine Greene, *Dialectic of Freedom*, 124.

26. Ibid., 129.

27. Ibid., 90.

28. Adrienne Rich, "Invisibility in Academe," quoted in Renato Rosaldo, *Culture and Truth: The Remaking of Social Analysis* (Boston: Beacon Press, 1989), ix.

BIBLIOGRAPHY

Ames, Nancy, and Edward Miller. *Changing Middle Schools: How to Make Schools Work for Young Adolescents.* San Francisco: Jossey-Bass, 1994.

Apple, Michael. *Official Knowledge: Democratic Education in a Conservative Age.* New York: Routledge, 1993.

Arcilla, Rene. "How Can the Misanthrope Learn? Philosophy for Education." In *Philosophy of Education 1994.* Urbana, IL: Philosophy of Education Society, 1995.

Banks, James. *An Introduction to Multicultural Education.* Boston: Allyn and Bacon, 1994.

Bellah, Robert, Richard Madsen, William Sullivan, Ann Swidler, and Steven Tipton. *Habits of the Heart: Individualism and Commitment in American Life.* New York: Harper and Row, 1986.

Benhabib, Seyla. *Situating the Self.* Cambridge, MA: Harvard University Press, 1993.

Berliner, David, and Bruce Biddle. *The Manufactured Crisis.* Reading, Mass: Addison-Wesley, 1995.

Blustein, Jeffrey. *Care and Commitment: Taking the Personal Point of View.* Oxford: Oxford University Press, 1991.

155

Boler, Megan. "The Risks of Empathy: Interrogating Multiculturalism's Gaze." *Proceedings of the Philosophy of Education 1994.* Urbana, IL: Philosophy of Education Society, 1995.

Bonstingl, John Jay. *Introduction to the Social Sciences.* Boston: Allyn and Bacon, 1980.

Braun, Eva. *Paradoxes of Education in a Republic.* Chicago: University of Chicago Press, 1979.

Brody, Howard. *Stories of Sickness.* New Haven: Yale University Press, 1989.

Bruner, Jerome. *Acts of Meaning.* Cambridge, MA: Harvard University Press, 1990.

Calkins, Lucy. *Living between the Lines.* Portsmouth, NH: Heinemann, 1991.

Callan, Eamonn. "Finding a Common Voice." In *Educational Theory,* (Fall 1992).

Carnegie Council on Adolescent Development. *Turning Points: Preparing American Youth for the Twenty-First Century.* Washington, DC: Carnegie Corporation, 1989.

Codrescu, Andrei. *Zombification.* New York: Picador, 1994.

Coles, Robert. *The Call of Stories: Teaching and the Moral Imagination.* Boston: Houghton-Mifflin, 1989.

————. *Privileged Ones: The Well-off and the Rich in America.* Boston: Little, Brown, 1977.

Collins, Patricia. *Black Feminist Thought: Knowledge, Consciousness, and the Politics of Empowerment.* New York: Routledge, 1991.

Comer, James P. "Educating Poor Minority Children." In *Scientific American* 259, no. 5, (November 1988).

Cookson, Peter, and Caroline Persell. *Preparing for Power: America's Elite Boarding Schools.* New York: Basic Books, 1985.

Counts, George S. *Dare the School Build a New Social Order?* Carbondale: Southern Illinois University Press, 1932.

Delpit, Lisa. *Other People's Children: Cultural Conflict in the Classroom.* New York: The New Press, 1995.

de Tocqueville, Alexis. *Democracy in America.* New York: Harper and Row, 1969.

Dewey, John. *Democracy and Education.* New York: The Free Press, 1916/1944.

————. "My Pedagogic Creed." In *Kaleidescope: Readings in Education,* edited by Ryan and Cooper. New York: Houghton-Mifflin, 1992.

Edelman, Marion. *Portrait of Inequality: Black and White Children in America.* Washington, DC: The Children's Defense Fund, 1980.

Egan, Kerry. *Teaching as Story-Telling: An Alternative Approach to Teaching and Curriculum in the Elementary School.* Chicago: University of Chicago Press, 1986.

Fleming, M., and J. McGinnis, eds. *Portraits: Biography and Autobiography in the Secondary School.* Urbana: National Council of Teachers of English, 1985.

Freire, Paulo. *Pedagogy of the Oppressed.* New York: Continuum, 1990.

Gadamer, Hans-Georg. *Truth and Method.* New York: Continuum, 1993.

Gay, Geneva. "Achieving Educational Equality through Curriculum Desegregation." *Phi Delta Kappan,* 72, no. 1, September 1990.

Gilligan, Carol. *In a Different Voice.* Cambridge, MA: Harvard University Press, 1982.

Goodlad, John. *A Place Called School.* New York: McGraw-Hill, 1984.

———. *What Schools Are For.* Phi Delta Kappa Educational Foundation, 1994.

Gould, Carol. *Rethinking Democracy.* New York: Cambridge University Press, 1988.

Graham, Patricia. *S.O.S.: Sustain Our Schools.* New York: Hill and Wang, 1992.

Green, Thomas S. "Public Speech." *18th Annual DeGarmo Lecture of the Society of Professors of Education.* San Francisco: Caddo Gap Press, 1993.

———. "Unwrapping the Ordinary: Philosophical Projects." *American Journal of Education* (November 1991).

Greene, Maxine. *The Dialectic of Freedom.* New York: Teachers College Press, 1988.

———. *Releasing the Imagination: Essays on Education, the Arts, and Social Change.* San Francisco: Jossey-Bass, 1995.

Gutierrez, Ramon. *When Jesus Came, the Corn Mothers Went Away.* Stanford: Stanford University Press, 1991.

Hafen, Bruce. "Developing Student Expression through Institutional Authority: Public Schools as Mediating Structures." *Ohio State Law Journal,* 48, (1987).

Hodgkin, Harold. "Reform versus Reality." *Phi Delta Kappan,* 73, no. 1 (September 1991).

Hoffman, Eva. *Lost in Translation.* New York: Penguin Books, 1989.

hooks, bell. *Teaching to Transgress: Education as the Practice of Freedom.* New York: Routledge, 1994.

———. *Yearning: Race, Gender, and Cultural Politics.* Boston: South End Press, 1990.

King, Jr., Martin Luther. *I Have a Dream: Writing and Speeches That Changed the World.* James Washington, ed. San Francisco: Harper San Francisco, 1992.

Kohl, Herbert. *I Won't Learn from You and Other Thoughts on Creative Maladjustment.* New York: The New Press, 1994.

———. *36 Children.* New York: New American Library, 1967/1988.

Kohn, Alfie. "Choices for Children: Why and How to Let Students Decide." *Phi Delta Kappan,* 75, no. 1 (September 1993).

Kozol, Jonathan. *Savage Inequalities: Children in America's Schools.* New York: Crown Publishers, 1991.

Kuhn, Thomas. *The Structure of Scientific Revolutions*. Chicago: University of Chicago Press, 1970.

Lasch, Christopher. *The Revolt of the Elites and the Betrayal of Democracy*. New York: W. W. Norton & Company, 1995.

Lazerson, Marvin. *An Education of Value*. Cambridge: Cambridge University Press, 1985.

Lewis, Anne. *Making It in the Middle: The Why and How of Excellent Schools for Young Urban Adolescents*. New York: The Edna McConnell Clark Foundation, 1990.

MacIntyre, Alasdair. *After Virtue*. Notre Dame: University of Notre Dame Press, 1981.

McLaughlin, Milbrey, Merita Irby, and Juliet Langman. *Urban Sanctuaries*. San Francisco: Jossey-Bass, 1994.

Martin, Jane. *The Schoolhome: Rethinking Schools for Changing Families*. Cambridge, MA: Harvard University Press, 1992.

Meier, Deborah, *The Power of Their Ideas: Lessons for America from a Small School in Harlem*. Boston: Beacon Press, 1995.

———. "Transforming Schools into Powerful Communities." *Teachers College Record* 94, no. 3 (Spring 1993).

Neusner, Jacob. *Telling Tales: Making Sense of Christian and Judaic Nonsense*. Louisville: Westminster Press, 1993.

Newton, Adam Zachary. *Narrative Ethics*. Cambridge, MA: Harvard University Press, 1995.

Noddings, Nel. *Caring: A Feminine Approach to Ethics and Moral Education*. Berkeley: The University of California Press, 1984.

Nussbaum, Martha. *Love's Knowledge: Essays on Philosophy and Literature*. New York: Oxford University Press, 1990.

Oldenburg, Ray. *The Great Good Place: Cafes, Coffee Shops, Community Centers, Beauty Parlors, General Stores, Bars, Hangouts and How They Get Us through the Day*. New York: Paragon House, 1989.

Paley, Vivian. *The Boy Who Would Be a Helicopter*. Cambridge, MA: Harvard University Press, 1990.

Pekarsky, Daniel. "Dehumanization and Education." In *Teachers College Record* 84, no. 2 (Winter 1987).

Percy, Walker. *Signposts in a Strange Land*. New York: Farrar, Straus and Giroux, 1991.

Polakow, Valerie. *Lives on the Edge: Single Mothers and Their Children in the Other America*. Chicago: University of Chicago Press, 1993.

Polkinghorne, Donald. *Narrative Knowing and the Human Sciences*. Albany: State University of New York Press, 1988.

Price, James, Charles Simpkinson, and Anne Simpkinson, eds. *Sacred Stories: A Celebration of the Power of Story to Transform and Heal*. San Francisco: HarperCollins, 1993.

Quint, Sharon. *Homeless Children: A Working Model for America's Public Schools*. New York: Teachers College Press, 1994.

Reed, Ronald, and Tony Johnson, eds. *Philosophical Documents in Education*. (New York: Longman Publishers USA, 1996).

Rich, Adrienne. "Invisibility in Academe." In *Culture and Truth: The Remaking of Social Analysis*, edited by Renato Rosaldo. Boston: Beacon Press, 1989.

Rodriguez, Richard. *Hunger of Memory*. New York: Bantam Books, 1982.

Rogers, Carl. *A Way of Being*. Boston: Houghton-Mifflin, 1980.

Roland, Alan. *In Search of Self in India and Japan: Towards a Cross-Cultural Psychology*. Princeton: Princeton University Press, 1988.

Rorty, Richard. *Contingency, Irony, and Solidarity*. Cambridge: Cambridge University Press, 1989.

Rosenwald, George, and Richard Ochberg, eds. *Storied Lives: The Cultural Politics of Self-Understanding*. New Haven: Yale University Press, 1992.

Ruddick, Sara. *Maternal Thinking: Toward a Politics of Peace*. Boston: Beacon Press, 1995.

Scott, James. *Domination and the Arts of Resistance*. New Haven: Yale University Press, 1990.

Searle, John. "How to Derive 'Ought' from 'Is.'" *The Philosophical Review* 73 (January 1964).

Shor, Ira. *Empowering Education: Critical Teaching for Social Change*. Chicago: The University of Chicago Press, 1992.

Spring, Joel. *American Education*. New York: Longman, 1991.

Taylor, Charles. *The Ethics of Authenticity*. Cambridge, MA: Harvard University Press, 1991.

————. *Multiculturalism: Examining the Politics of Recognition*. Princeton: Princeton University Press, 1994.

Toulmin, Stephen. *The Uses of Argument*. Cambridge: Cambridge University Press, 1958.

Tunnel, M. and R. Ammon, eds. *The Story of Ourselves: Teaching History through Children's Literature*. Portsmouth, NH: Heinemann, 1993.

Tyack, David, and Elizabeth Hansot. "Conflict and Consensus in American Education." *Daedalus*, 110 (1981).

Weiss, Lois. *Beyond Silenced Voices: Class, Race, and Gender in United States Schools*. Albany: State University of New York Press, 1993.

Wiersma, Jacquelyn. "Karen: The Transforming Story." In *Storied Lives: The Cultural Politics of Self-Understanding*, edited by Rosenwald and Ochberg. New Haven: Yale University Press, 1992.

Witherell, Carol, and Nel Noddings, eds. *Stories Lives Tell: Narrative and Dialogue in Education.* New York: Teachers College Press, 1991.

Wood, George. *Schools That Work.* New York: Plume Books, 1992.

Wright, Richard. *Black Boy.* New York: Harper and Row, 1937/1966.

INDEX

161